Prayers from a Grandma's Heart

ASKING GOD'S BLESSING AND PROTECTION
FOR YOUR GRANDCHILDREN

by Quin Sherrer

inspirio.

To my children
Quinett Rae,
Keith Alan,
Sherry Ruth

And to their children, my grandchildren
Kara Nicole
Evangeline Noel
Ethan Keil
Lyden Benjamin
Victoria Jewett
Samuel Johannes

May you always put your trust in God!

❧ Table of Contents

Prayers *from a* Grandma's Heart

I have been reminded of your sincere faith, which first lived in your grandmother Lois and in your mother Eunice and, I am persuaded, now lives in you also.

2 Timothy 1:5

When the Apostle Paul wrote these words to his spiritual son, Timothy, he acknowledged the powerful influence of Timothy's godly grandmother, Lois, encouraging him to imitate her faith and character. Today we grandmothers continue to have an enormous influence on the spiritual well-being of our grandchildren. Even children who are reared in a Christian home need someone to pray tenaciously for them, and who can do it better than a grandma?

Prayers from a Grandma's Heart is designed as a heartening guide, offering stories of encouragement and easy-to-read prayers for every grandchild's needs, no matter his or her age. Divided into various categories, this book will help you find appropriate prayers for each season and situation in your grandchild's life.

Prayers from a Grandma's Heart is created to help you pray God's blessings and promises for each grandchild. As you pray what Scripture says, God's power is released into your grandchild's life. It is our hope that this book will help you as a grandmother assume a role of increasing spiritual influence in your grand-children's lives, no matter what difficulties they may be facing.

We will tell the next generation
the praiseworthy deeds of the LORD,
his power, and the wonders he has done.
He decreed statutes for Jacob
and established the law in Israel,
which he commanded our forefathers
to teach their children,
so the next generation would know them,
even the children yet to be born,
and they in turn would tell their children.
Then they would put their trust in God
and would not forget his deeds
but would keep his commands.

Psalm 78:4–7

Praying from a Grandma's Heart

*I thank God, . . . as night and day I
constantly remember you in my prayers.*
2 Timothy 1:3

In Luke 18, Jesus tells a story about a woman who persistently
plead her case with the judge of her village until he finally
heard and answered her request. He uses this story to
encourage his disciples to be persistent and faithful in
bringing their requests to God. He assures him that unlike the
judge, who only granted the woman's request because he was
annoyed with her persistence, God will grant our requests
because he loves us. "Will not God bring about justice for his
chosen ones, who cry out to him day and night? Will he keep
putting them off? I tell you, he will see that they get justice,
and quickly" (Luke 18:7-8).

As grandmothers we can be encouraged by the words of Jesus
to continue praying every day for our grandchildren. God will
be faithful to answer our prayers for our treasured ones.

My Mom's Prayers

My own mom was not only my prime prayer warrior, but she was also a great intercessor for my three children, her grandchildren. Although Mother had always prayed and attended church on Sunday—and took us with her—she developed an even greater desire to pray after a spiritual renewal when she was sixty-two. By then she had retired and had ten grandchildren spanning in age from crib to junior high.

Whenever you'd ask Mom, "What's your greatest joy?" she'd wave both hands toward heaven and say, "To praise the Lord and to pray for my ten grandchildren represented by these ten fingers." When they were lonely, depressed, or in need of prayer, my children often called her from college with requests such as, "Mother Jewett, I've got such a hard test Friday. I'm uptight about it. Please pray for me to have peace and to remember everything I've studied." Mom would bombard heaven on behalf of that grandchild.

She seemed to have spiritual insights about our children that we didn't always have. She also felt free to tell us when she thought we should put actions to our prayers. Once after talking to our son, who admitted he was having difficulty making his checkbook balance, Mom told us, "You all need to go to that Florida State campus and see your two kids—if for nothing more than to encourage them with your presence."

My husband couldn't get off work to go, so I left the next day for Tallahassee with his blessings and some money for our college senior from his grandmother to make his bank account solvent. I've no idea how many hours Mom prayed for my children—only God knows.

While caring for Mom as she was dying of cancer, I read Scriptures to her during the long nights when she couldn't sleep. Once while reading Proverbs 13:22, "A good man leaves an inheritance for his children's children," she told me, "I want to leave them a spiritual inheritance."

"You've done that already," I assured her.

When I read Proverbs 17:6, "Children's children are a crown to the aged," she managed to say, "My grandchildren are truly my crown right now."

Just before our son graduated, Mom died. After commencement ceremonies, as we stood outside, our son clutched his diploma to his chest and looked up toward heaven. "I miss my grandmother so much. I wish she could have been here today. She helped me earn this with her prayers."

Prayer can impact our grandchildren's lives. Our Father, who created each of His children uniquely different, loves to hear us talk to Him, especially about our children's children. As grandmoms we have the priceless privilege to do that every day.

Prayers for the Privilege of Praying for my Grandchildren

Lord, thank you for the privilege of coming to You daily on behalf of my grandchildren. How I love them. Yet I know You love them even more. Help me to pray what's on your heart for them. Enable me to be a godly grandmother, one they will want to imitate. I desire to leave them a spiritual inheritance that they can pass on to their children. Show me ways to bless them in words and actions.

Lord, out of your unlimited goodness, I ask You to impart supernatural favor and blessing, prosperity, and happiness upon my grandchildren.

*Thank you that You will pour out your
Spirit on my offspring, and Your blessings
on my descendants—and that includes
my grandchildren.*
(Isaiah 44:3)

~

*I thank my God every time I remember
my grandchildren. In all my prayers for all
of them, I always pray with joy.*
(Philippians 1:3–4)

~

*Thank you, Lord that I can pray for my
grandchildren, holding fast to the confession
of my hope without wavering, for
He who promises is faithful.*
(Hebrews 10:23)

~

Scriptures for Meditation

Know therefore that the LORD your God is God;
he is the faithful God, keeping his covenant of
love to a thousand generations of those who
love him and keep his commands.
Deuteronomy 7:9

࿘

From everlasting to everlasting
  the LORD's love is with those who fear him,
  and his righteousness with their children's
    children —
with those who keep his covenant
and remember to obey his precepts.
Psalm 103:17–18

࿘

Bestowing the Blessing

In addition to praying regularly for your grand-children, you can bless them, too. In their book, *The Blessing*, authors Gary Smalley and John Trent say that a family blessing includes the following:

- *A meaningful touch*
- *A spoken message*
- *Attaching "high value" to the one being blessed*
- *An active commitment to fulfill the blessing*

According to Smalley and Trent, the verb "to bless" means to show reverence or to esteem a person valuable. To bless in the biblical sense also means to ask for or to impart *supernatural favor*. When we ask God to *bless* our grandchildren, we are crying out for the wonderful, unlimited goodness that only God has the power to give to them. How loved children must feel to have grandparents pray over them, bless them, and impart love in a special way.

My husband and I have a yearly "blessing service" at our daughter's home—to bless our six little grandchildren, all under the age of seven. They wait in line for their turn for Papa LeRoy and Mama Quin to lay hands on their heads and pray. As their grandparents, we ask God to invoke His blessings on them. We speak a special blessing appropriate to each one separately, as did the biblical patriarch Jacob who prayed over his grandsons and children (Genesis 48:15-16; 49:28). After a personal prayer, we read Scriptures aloud over them. Then we bless our grandchildren with this final verse from Numbers 6:24-26:

> The LORD bless you
>   and keep you;
> the LORD make his face shine upon you
>   and be gracious to you;
> the LORD turn his face toward you
>   and give you peace.

Four of our grandchildren were dedicated to the Lord right after their births at the homes of our children. Both sets of grandparents gathered with the parents to pray blessings from the Bible over the little ones and pledge before God to do our part to help influence these children in the ways of the Lord as they mature.

Grandma Tina wrote this prayer for her young grandson, pasted his picture on one side and had it made into a laminated bookmark to keep in her Bible for daily prayer for him.

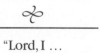

"Lord, I …

*Pray that his little eyes will
see the good things of life.*

*Pray that his little ears are sensitive
to the voice of the Holy Spirit.*

*Pray that his little hands
are holy unto the Lord.*

*Pray that his words
are loving, kind, and gentle.*

*Pray that he will always obey
and honor his parents.*

*Pray that God's Holy Word
will always be in his heart.*

Pray that he will live a long and happy life.

I pray in Jesus' name, Amen."

A Grandchild's Story

Grandmothers can provide prayer models for children in a society where intergenerational bonding is so badly needed. Not only can the younger ones hear their grandmothers pray, but they can come to expect them to pray for them whenever they need prayer.

I pray with my preschool grandchildren whenever the opportunity arises. When they spend the night with us, as I'm tucking them in for the night, I sit on the bed and pray specifically for them. Then they each pray aloud in their own child-like phrases—praying for everything from parents and friends to their cat Bailey.

Recently, when my four-year-old granddaughter Evangeline got stung by a bee three times on her face, my son dialed my telephone number for her so she could ask her grandmother to pray away her pain. As she sobbed, she told me how badly she hurt.

Of course I prayed aloud right then, joining my prayers with her daddy's, who at that moment was struggling to comfort her on their way to the pharmacy.

A few nights later I was sleeping across the room from my five-year-old-grandson Lyden Benjamin when he awoke from a nightmare. "Mama Quin, how do I get those monsters to go away?" he asked, sitting upright in his bed.

"Just ask Jesus to make them go away," I answered.

"Oh, OK—is that all?" he asked. I prayed and he repeated after me, then he rolled over and fell asleep again.

Grandchildren just seem to trust their grandmas. And grandmas trust their God!

Praying for Salvation and Spiritual Growth

God so loved the world that he gave his one and only Son, that whoever believes in him shall not perish but have eternal life.
John 3:16

As a grandmother, you hold a special place in the hearts and minds of your grandchildren. You can share your knowledge, love, and faith with them. And you can use your influence to steer them in the ways of the Lord, always encouraging them in their spiritual journey as they mature in the things of God.

The most important prayer we grandmas can pray is for our grandchildren to receive Christ as Savior. Then we can pray for the opportunity for us or someone else to share the simple Gospel with them, and finally, that they in turn will be used by God to influence their generation for Christ, too.

Grandma Sally's Legacy

Immediately following Grandma Sally's funeral, a host
of her grandchildren joined their parents in returning to
the old homestead to celebrate her life. They sang from
memory many of her favorite hymns. Then they listened
to a cassette tape the ninety-six-year-old family matriarch
had recorded in an effort to pass down some of her
homespun wisdom and poetry, and a short account
of her spiritual journey, to her descendants. Jennie,
a granddaughter who was touched when she heard her
grandmother's voice said, "I suddenly realized I am a
believer because of Grandma
Sally's prayers. She lived so far
from our family I only saw her
every few years, but at this
gathering after her funeral I
knew for certain she had prayed
for all of us. She used to say to
me, 'God bless you, darling,' then
she'd encourage me with
a Bible verse."

Grandmother Janie Leads Jess to Christ

Whenever little Jess visited his Grandmother Janie,
she read him Bible stories and took him to church with
her. The summer he turned nine he was excited to
be able to attend Vacation Bible School at her church.

 One afternoon toward the end of
the week, as they talked in her guest
bedroom, Grandmother Janie sensed
that Jess's heart was tender and
open for her to talk to him about
developing a personal relationship
with the Lord. After she read a few
verses from the Bible to him, she
asked, "Wouldn't you like to know
Jesus—to ask Him to come live in
your life?"

"Yes," he replied immediately. His grandmother prayed
a simple prayer which he repeated. "*Lord, Jesus, I need
You. I want You to be my Savior all the days of my life.
Forgive me for all the wrongs I've done. Help me to
please You in everything I do and say. Thank you that
I will live with You in heaven someday. Amen.*"

Jess seemed to understand the things of God right away. Though he lived in Chicago and his grandmother in New York, she prayed with him frequently over the phone. Living in a home with an unbelieving step-dad and a mother who didn't encourage  him in spiritual things was sometimes hard for Jess. But he would always call his Grandmother Janie to pray for the various challenges he faced.

Today Jess is seventeen, and he's never wavered in his love for Jesus. He's been on overseas mission trips and is active in his church's youth group. His grandmother recognizes qualities in him of a budding spiritual leader.

Prayers for My Grandchildren's Salvation

Lord, I pray for my grandchildren to come to a saving knowledge of Jesus at an early age. I pray they will stay within the boundaries of Your love and safety. Lord, You instruct us to tell the next generations about Your marvelous works, that our offspring's offspring would know You, put their confidence in You and keep Your commandments.

Show me what to say to my grandchildren in a letter, a phone call, or face to face conversation, about all the wonderful things You have done for our family. I want so much to encourage them to love You always and trust You with their present circumstances as well as their future. I pray that my grandchildren will encounter God in an ongoing, ever-expanding, and life-changing way. Amen.

Lord, Your Word says that if we confess with our mouth that Jesus is Lord and believe in our hearts that God raised Him from the dead, we shall be saved. For it is with the heart that we believe and are justified, and it is with our mouths that we confess and are saved. This is my heart's desire for all my grandchildren. I thank you in advance that this will become a reality and that they will spend eternity with You.
(Romans 10:9–10)

Give my grandchildren opportunities to hear the Gospel and open hearts to receive Your gift of salvation—Jesus Christ. Keep their eyes opened to truth, and their hearts protected from deception. Thank you, Lord, for being patient with us, not wanting anyone to perish, but everyone to come to repentance. May my grandchildren come to that repentance and gain an early knowledge of the Savior who is Christ.
(2 Peter 3:9)

Prayers for My Grandchildren's Spiritual Growth

I pray that my grandchildren will love the Lord God with all their hearts, souls, minds, and strength, and love their neighbors as themselves—the two great commandments Jesus gave us (Mark 12:30–31). Help them learn to discern when You are speaking to them. Fuel them with passion and excitement for the things of God concerning their individual lives. May they experience Your presence daily.

Help my grandchildren to read the Bible and understand it. As they meditate upon it, it will provide food for their spiritual growth and instruction for their daily living (Psalm 1:2).

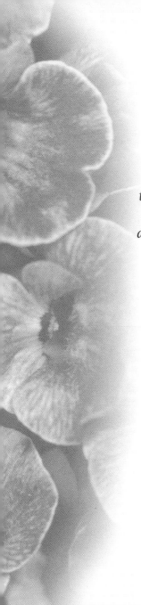

Lord, I thank you that You work in my grandchildren—to will and to act according to Your good purpose. Help them keep in mind that they are God's workmanship, created in Christ Jesus to do good works, which God prepared in advance for them to do. Help them in their spiritual growth, to keep on growing in their faith.
(Philippians 2:13; Ephesians 2:10)

Lord, I stand with faith upon what Your word says my grandchildren can become. Thank you for the promises that You will reach out and touch our offspring's offspring, generation after generation.
(Deuteronomy 7:9)

Scriptures for Meditation

Everyone who calls
on the name of the Lord shall be saved.
Acts 2:21

Little children were brought to Jesus for
him to place his hands on them and pray
for them. But the disciples rebuked those
who brought them. Jesus said, "Let the
little children come to me, and do not
hinder them, for the kingdom of heaven
belongs to such as these."
Matthew 19:13–14

Prayer for Salvation to Pray with My Grandchildren

Lord Jesus, I'm sorry for the things I've done that have hurt You and other people. Please forgive me. I want to receive You as my Savior. I believe You are the Son of God, who came to earth, died on the cross, shed Your blood for my sins, and rose from the dead. Thank you for opening the way for me to pray to God the Father in Your name. Thank you for the promise of eternal life with You. Thank you for loving me unconditionally. Now help me to please You as Lord of my life. Amen.

What Salvation Means:

_____

There is a God. (Romans 1:20)

*God loves you and wants you to
know Him. (John 3:16)*

*Our wrong doings have kept us from
knowing God. (Romans 3:23)*

Eternal life is a free gift. (Romans 6:23)

*You can receive this gift now by
believing in Jesus. (Romans 10:9)*

*Once you believe, you become a child
of God. (John 1:12)*

_____

A Grandchild's Story

Grandmother Beth's three-year-old granddaughter Angel was explaining Easter to her over the phone. She told Grandma all about what Jesus endured—the beatings, the horrible death on the cross, and being buried in the tomb with a stone to seal the entrance.

Excitedly she told how He burst out of that tomb and was on earth with His friends for some days before He finally went to heaven to be with His Father, God.

"He did that all for me, Nonnie," she explained. "Guess what He's doing now?"

"You tell me, Angel."

"Well, He is sitting down—right next to God, and He's praying for me. But Nonnie, if you'd been through all He went through you'd want to sit down too, wouldn't you?"

Grandmother Beth chuckled to herself. Pretty good Gospel message, she thought. Yes, even a three-year-old can comprehend the simple story of salvation.

Praying for Divine Protection

You are my hiding place, O Lord;
*   you will protect me from trouble*
and surround me with songs of deliverance.
Psalm 32:7

Grandmas' prayers naturally focus around the daily safety of their grandchildren, including their physical, spiritual, and emotional well-being. Our hearts plead for God's protecting hand to be upon the precious ones He's brought into our family. We can even begin to pray for our grandchildren before they are born.

A career woman writes about a special grandmother whose prayers affected her life.

"If I were to acknowledge anyone who has helped me understand prayer it would be my great-grandmother, Olean. Without her prayers, I might never have been born. My mother was in difficult labor for three days, but my great-grandmother prayed day and night until I was finally born early on a Sunday morning. Her prayers continued to follow me all my life until her death. Like a heavenly search light her prayers exposed darkness in my life, yet at other times they gave me the hope I needed while going through a difficult situation."

Prayers for My Unborn Grandchild

Lord, I'm so excited. A new grandbaby is on the way.
Thank you for creating this child. May You always be
near to help and watch over her—all the days of her life.

Fill this child with Your Presence. Endow her with health
and happiness. Help her grow according to Your plan of
development. Fill this precious little one with a great
desire to be born and an
excitement for the things You have
in store for her—spiritually and
physically.

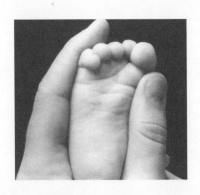

Lord, you created my unborn grandchild.
You knit him together in his mother's womb.
I praise you because he is fearfully and wonderfully
made; your works are wonderful, I know that full well.
Your eyes see his unformed body. All his days are
ordained for him, written in your book before
one of them comes to be.
(Psalm 139:13–16)

Prayers for My Grandchildren's Protection

*Lord, keep my grandchildren from all harm—
watch over their lives;
Lord, watch over their coming and going
both now and forevermore.*
(Psalm 121:7–8)

*Lord, I pray for the physical protection of my
grandchildren. I commit them into Your care
and safekeeping. I'm standing on the biblical
promise that because my grandchildren love You,
You will rescue and protect them. When they
call upon You, You will answer them, and be
with them in trouble and deliver them.*
(Psalm 91:14–15)

*Lord, I thank you that my grandchildren can
go on their way in safety. When they lie down,
they will not be afraid, and their sleep will be
sweet. They will have no fear of sudden disaster
for You are their confidence, and You will
keep them from being snared.*
(Proverbs 3:23–26)

My own family experienced the joy of seeing God's divine protection firsthand one day:

When they came in my front door, my daughter and her two small children were breathing quite heavily and all were talking at the same time. "A wreck, a wreck, just one car ahead of us—just one block before we got here . . . we could have been crushed, it was such a close call." My daughter's four-year-old told me excitedly, "We prayed. We called on Jesus." I then told them how just that morning Papa LeRoy and I had prayed longer than usual for God to protect all our grandchildren, asking Him to have His angels watch over them. How thankful we were to Him for answering our prayer in such a powerful way that very afternoon.

Prayers for My Grandchildren's Emotional Protection

Bless all my grandchildren with the knowledge
of Your presence, Lord. Let them know they can call
on You—even in a time of trouble. May they learn to
trust in You completely. You will deliver them and
satisfy them with long life and show them Your salvation.
Lord, You have been our dwelling place throughout
all generations. May this cycle continue in the lives
of my grandchildren and their children.
(Psalm 50:15; 91:16; 90:1)

God, be my grandchildren's refuge and strength,
an ever-present help in trouble, so they will not fear.
LORD Almighty be with them. Be their fortress.
(Psalm 46:1–2, 7)

Lord, help my grandchildren not to fear or be
dismayed for You are their God. You will strengthen
and help my grandchildren. You will uphold them with
Your righteous right hand.
(Isaiah 41:10)

Prayers for My Grandchildren's Spiritual Protection

Lord, thank you that You are faithful to strengthen my grandchildren and protect them from the evil one. May the Lord direct their hearts into God's love and Christ's perseverance.
(2 Thessalonians 3:3, 5)

⌒

Lord, I thank you that You will always be my grandchildren's Shepherd. They shall not want. You restore their souls and guide them in paths of righteousness. Even though they may walk through the valley of the shadow of death, they will fear no evil, for You are with them. You comfort them. You prepare a table before them in the presence of their enemies. You anoint their head with oil and their cup overflows. Surely goodness and love will follow them all the days of their lives. And they will dwell in the house of the Lord forever.
(Psalm 23)

⌒

Prayers for My Grandchildren's Safety in Body, Mind and Spirit

Lord, I pray that my grandchildren will make You, the Most High their dwelling—even the Lord, who is their refuge. For You, God, will command your angels concerning them, to guard them in all their ways.
(Psalm 91:9, 11)

The Lord is my grandchild's helper, he will not be afraid. What can man do to him?
(Hebrews 13:6)

Scriptures for Meditation

The name of the LORD is a strong tower;
the righteous run to it and are safe.
Proverbs 18:10

In the day of trouble
God will keep me safe in his dwelling;
he will hide me in the shelter of his
tabernacle
and set me high upon a rock.
Psalm 27:5

Praise be to the LORD,
for he has heard my cry for mercy.
The LORD is my strength and my shield;
my heart trusts in him, and
I am helped.
Psalm 28:6–7

A Grandchild's Story

"Do we get to ride in the red wagon and sing today?"
my four-year-old grandson asked me.

"Sure, as soon as it warms up we'll take a stroll,"
I assured him.

A couple of hours later, I had three grandchildren, all
under five years of age, bundled up for our ride. To the
ordinary observer I was pulling my little grandchildren
in a little red wagon through a three block area in our
neighborhood. But in reality we were on a "prayer walk."
Our goal is to pray for protection for our neighborhood,
to ask for God's peace on our neighbors, and for all of
them to come to know Jesus personally.

As we bump down the street, I pray aloud, then we sing,
sometimes making up verses to go with popular tunes
the children know. I first started my neighborhood
"prayer walking" as soon as the first grandchild came
home from the hospital and his mother asked me to
take him strolling. I'd sing or hum the chorus "Allelujah,"
and he soon learned to do it too.

Before long I had several grandchildren, all toddlers, living nearby. We graduated from strollers to the little red wagon. Now when the weather is pleasant we sometimes see neighbors sitting in their yards who greet us and we stop to talk.

They love to hear the songs the little ones sing—even off-key—and sometimes they comment on the Bible tunes. *Jesus Loves the Little Children, Joshua Fought the Battle of Jericho, Father Abraham,* and on and on. As we sing, walk and talk, I usually give my grandchildren a lesson tied in with the Bible song we are singing.

Once after the police arrested some gang members just down the street from us, I realized more than ever the need to pray for protection over our neighborhood.

But as I teach my grandchildren to pray for peace and protection, I do it without instilling fear. I'm hoping that they become alert to pray and care for their own neighborhoods.

One day when I commented that a mother living in one house needed special prayer because her son was in jail, my almost five-year-old grandson asked, "What did he do? Did he bow down to some golden idol like Daniel and his friends were told to do, but they didn't?"

"No, not that," I said. "He just had a different idol in his heart, and he disobeyed the law."

Walking my neighborhood has deepened my grand-children's prayer life. But it has also stretched mine to a new capacity, because I need to ask God to show me how to pray each time I take them for a stroll and then share with them what is on His heart.

The fruit of the Spirit is love, joy, peace, patience, kindness, goodness, faithfulness, gentleness and self control. Against such things there is no law.
Galatians 5:22–23

After our grandchildren develop a personal relationship with Jesus, we should continue to ask God to help them develop the fruit of the Holy Spirit in their lives. We should pray too that they respond to God's grace instead of developing a legalistic understanding of their faith.

Often our grandchildren's character is further developed as they spend quality time with grandparents, storing up happy memories that influence them years later. You may work fulltime or just don't live close by, but even if you only have the opportunity to spend time with your grandchildren once a year, you can make a difference.

Special Weekend Together

Though she prays daily for her granddaughter Nicole, Grandmother Mary spends one special weekend alone each year with Nicole in a hotel for their personal retreat. She's done this since her granddaughter turned five— some ten years ago.

Mary and Nicole check into a hotel, go shopping, swimming, and out for dinner in a nice restaurant. Then they return to their hotel where they talk for hours about things of interest to Nicole, from her school projects to prayer for her future husband.

Mary says, "As I pray aloud for my granddaughter, I ask God to prepare her for her future, just as my Christian grandmother did for me as a young girl."

When the storms of life occur, Mary knows Nicole will be aware that the Lord's arms are around her and will sustain her even as her grandmother's arms have been around her, praying for her all these years. Nicole's character has blossomed so beautifully as she has begun to apply some of the biblical principles she has learned from her grandmother. Nicole and Mary talk on the phone or get together on other occasions also, to share, and for Grandmother Mary to inquire how she can pray more specifically for Nicole.

Prayers for My Grandchildren's Character Development

Lord, I pray that my grandchildren will always maintain integrity and honesty. Please help them develop the fruit of the Spirit in their lives—love, joy, peace, patience, kindness, goodness, faithfulness, gentleness and self-control. Only You, Lord, can do that. Amen.

Lord, help my grandchildren to develop godly character by living a life worthy of the Lord and pleasing You in every way, bearing fruit in every good work and growing in the knowledge of God. May they be strengthened with all power according to Your glorious might so that they may have great endurance and patience. Help my grandchildren to be imitators of God and live lives of love.
(Colossians 1:10–11; Ephesians 5:1-2)

As my grandchildren's characters are continually developed and refined, I pray they will not be conformed to the pattern of this world, but be transformed by the renewing of their minds. Then they will be able to test and approve what God's will is—His good, pleasing and perfect will.
(Romans 12:2)

Love

In a time when the youth culture seems bent on encouraging children to pursue a self-centered "I-me-mine" attitude, it is so important for grandmas to pray that their grandchildren will instead develop a "love attitude" for other people. As a grandmother we can think of hundreds of ways to teach our grandchildren to love, but more importantly, we can pray they will "grow to love" as their compassion and understanding of others expands. Only God can help them to achieve this deeply needed characteristic. Paul, the apostle, said, "Love is patient, love is kind. ... It always protects, always trusts, always hopes, always perseveres. Love never fails." (1 Corinthians 13:4, 7–8). Let's pray our grandchildren will personally experience and demonstrate this kind of love.

Father, we love because God first loved us. You are the epitome of love. As the Creator, You placed the "love capacity" in our hearts with which to love. In turn, please help my grandchildren to know and express that kind of pure love.

Lord, help my grandchildren love with unselfish love. Enable them to love with actions and in truth. For love is patient, love is kind. It does not envy, it does not boast, it is not proud. It is not rude, it is not self-seeking, it is not easily angered, it keeps no record of wrongs. Love does not delight in evil but rejoices with the truth. It always protects, always trusts, always hopes, always perseveres. Love never fails. Lord, I pray that my grandchildren's love may abound still more and more—for You and for others You bring across their paths. For I know in this they will experience joy!

(1 John 3:18; 1 Corinthians 13:4–8; Philippians 1:9)

Joy

Joy does not depend on happiness or pleasant circumstances. Rather as someone once said, "joy is an attitude of gratitude." Joy, when grounded in commitment to God, sees things from His point of view. We can pray for and encourage our grandchildren to be joyful for every day, for every blessing, every friendship, everything God has given them to enjoy. Since joy is mentioned more than 200 times in the Bible, it must be pretty important in God's eyes.

Lord, it's my heart's desire that my grandchildren will continually rejoice in You—keeping their faith anchored in Jesus, the Rock. May joy bubble up from deep within them. Help them laugh at the impossible and believe You for the answers.

Lord, Your Word says the joy of the Lord is our strength. Help my grandchildren learn how to know joy regardless of situations and disappointments, victories or defeats they encounter. Flood my grandchildren with Your love and joy.
(Nehemiah 8:10)

Lord, help my grandchildren to be joyful always; pray continually; and give thanks in all circumstances, for this is God's will for them in Christ Jesus.
(1 Thessalonians 5:16–18)

Peace

Peace. It is something the whole world talks about, dreams about and hopes to obtain. It's a calmness, an absence of strife. Yet only God, who reconciled us to Himself through Jesus, His son, gives us inner peace. How we long for our grandchildren to experience His presence, His peace, His quietness of soul.

Lord, I am asking You to bestow peace on my grandchildren today. Only You can give inner peace of mind, soul, spirit. Only You can steady them and bring calm, serenity, quiet, and rest to them. When their hearts are troubled, when plans go haywire, when others let them down, help them know and rely on Your peace— a peace that passes understanding, O Lord.

Now may the Lord of peace himself give my grandchildren peace at all times, and in every way. The Lord be with them always.
(2 Thessalonians 3:16)

Thank you for Jesus' own promises, "Peace I leave with you, my peace I give you. I do not give to you as the world gives. Do not let your hearts be troubled and do not be afraid". Envelop my grandchildren with Your peace, O Prince of Peace.
(John 14:27)

Patience

Patience often requires the virtue of waiting, enduring, persevering, and seeking serenity. Our grandchildren, like us, must continually work at being patient when things around us would give us cause to come unglued.

Lord, teach my grandchildren how to practice and achieve patience—in every arena of their lives. Help them keep calm, quiet, unruffled, and remain anger-free at the people or situations that gave them reason to be impatient.

Help my grandchildren to be still and know that you are God; may they know that they can and should rest in the Lord and wait patiently for You, just as the psalmist did. You inclined to him, and heard his cry. So teach my grandchildren how to wait patiently for you to hear their petitions and move on their behalf.
(Psalm 46:10; 37:7; 40:1)

Kindness

Grandmothers, with hearts full of compassion, love to shower kindnesses on their grandchildren through encouraging words and helpful deeds. Grandma Sheryl took her seventeen-year-old grandson Chad, for his driver's license test, promising to pray for him during the test. It turned out to be an all-afternoon event. Finally, when Chad had finished his test and learned he had passed, Grandma was there to congratulate him. As he drove her car home, they stopped at his favorite donut shop to celebrate. What a memorable afternoon they shared as Grandma showered him with her time, consideration, and kindness. Not only did she pray for Chad to have a kind heart, she was setting an example for him to follow in extending kindness, too.

Lord, help my grandchildren respond with kindness in whatever situations they encounter. Help them develop and express kindness in their homes, schools, and workplaces. Instill in them empathy, consideration, and concern for others. Give them creative ways to show acts of kindness.

Lord, I pray when my grandchildren open their mouths they will speak with wisdom, and may the teaching of kindness be on their tongues.
(Proverbs 31:26, NASB)

Goodness

Goodness, as expressed in the Bible, has various meanings: genuine, honorable, dependable, honest. In today's language goodness makes us think of someone who is morally excellent, virtuous, or well behaved. All of these are admirable character traits to pray for our grandchildren to develop.

Lord, I pray that my grandchildren will be dependable, well behaved, morally excellent, virtuous, and honorable. Work into their character the fruit of goodness, and teach them how to respond with that goodness and love to a hurting world in need of You. Lord, may my grandchildren always choose what is good.

Lord, help my grandchildren make every effort to add to their faith goodness; and to goodness, knowledge; and to knowledge, self-control; and to self-control, perseverance; and to perseverance, godliness; and to godliness, brotherly kindness; and to brotherly kindness, love.
(2 Peter 1:5–7)

As my grandchildren have opportunity, let them do good to all people, Lord, I pray.
(Galatians 6:10)

Faithfulness

A faithful person is trustworthy in his promises, obligations, or performance. You can count on his word. God's Word says if we are faithful in even the little things in life, we will be faithful in much. God rewards faithfulness. When we and our grandchildren stand before our Father in heaven, how we want the Master to welcome us with, "Well done, good and faithful servants!" (Matthew 25:23).

Lord God, help my grandchildren develop faithfulness in their character. May they be:

- *Faithful to friends*
- *Faithful to keep their word*
- *Faithful to love God*
- *Faithful to finish the tasks they start.*

LORD, thank you that as my grandchildren are
faithful they will be richly blessed, for you reward
every person for his righteousness and faithfulness.
(Proverbs 28:20; 1 Samuel 26:23)

Thank you, Lord, that you say those who are
faithful with very little can be trusted with much.
May my grandchildren be trustworthy and faithful
in all they undertake.
(Luke 16:10)

Gentleness

A tender heart. A soft touch. A quiet and loving response. Caring more about another's feelings than of one's own rights. The Apostle Peter wrote that a gentle and quiet spirit is an imperishable quality, precious in God's sight (1 Peter 3:4).

Lord, help my grandchildren keep a gentle and meek spirit, to be loving toward others, and forgiving, outgoing and caring in tender ways.

Thank you that Jesus said, "Blessed are the gentle for they shall inherit the earth." May this promise be so in the lives of my grandchildren.
(Matthew 5:5, NASB)

Lord, Your Word says, "A gentle answer turns away wrath, but a harsh word stirs up anger." So I ask that you help my grandchildren respond with gentleness when speaking to others.
(Proverbs 15:1)

Self-Control

The Apostle Paul understood the struggle to maintain self-control, "I know that nothing good lives in me, that is, in my sinful nature. For I have the desire to do what is good, but I cannot carry it out" (Romans 7:18). Paul goes on to say that the only way he can overcome is through the Holy Spirit—to let God work in him to overcome his sinful nature. We grandmothers should pray that the Holy Spirit will help our grandchildren in the same way.

God, help my grandchildren appropriate Your power and practice self-control.

Lord, help my grandchildren live in harmony with others, to be sympathetic, loving as brothers, compassionate and humble, not repaying evil with evil or insult with insult, but with blessing, because to this they were called so that they may inherit a blessing.
(1 Peter 3:8–9)

Help my grandchildren be slow to speak and slow to become angry, for man's anger does not bring about the righteous life that God desires.
(James 1:19–20)

Self-Esteem

*Help my grandchildren develop good self-esteem as
they realize that they are God's workmanship, created
in Christ Jesus to do good works.*
(Ephesians 2:10)

Courage

*May my grandchildren always be strong and courageous
in their character and actions because You, O Lord,
go with them and will never leave them.*
(Deuteronomy 31:6)

Justice

*Enable my grandchildren to love justice
as you do. May they act justly, love mercy
and walk humbly with their God.*
(Psalm 11:7; Micah 6:8)

Respect

*Help my grandchildren show proper respect
to everyone, as your word commands.*
(1 Peter 2:17)

A Grandchild's Story

"Excuse me, Mama Quin, I have to go off and be by myself a while," five-year-old Lyden told me, with a scowl on his face. A little while later he came back smiling.

"What was that all about?" I asked.

"Well, my mom says when I get angry I have to give all my anger to Jesus—and He forgives me. He wants me to change my heart's attitude. When Sissy took my toy, I got mad, but I knew I couldn't stay that way."

Now whenever he is visiting grandmother and I see anger rising up in him, I suggest he take a time-out to talk to the Lord about it. Sometimes he prays aloud; other times he asks me to pray and he adds his "amen." On these times, I see that my prayers for the development of his character are being answered.

*This is my prayer: that your love may
abound more and more in knowledge
and depth of insight, so that you may be
able to discern what is best and may be
pure and blameless until the day of Christ,
filled with the fruit of righteousness
that comes through Jesus Christ—
to the glory and praise of God.*
Philippians 1:9–11

Praying for My Grandchildren's Parents

May the LORD make you increase,
* both you and your children.*
May you be blessed by the LORD,
* the Maker of heaven and earth.*
Psalm 115:14

As grandparents we can be prayer warriors for our grand-children's parents, too. Our children, now parents themselves, need to hear our words of encouragement, affirmation, and they especially need our prayers.

It's difficult being a parent today. There are outside forces pulling on mothers, fathers, boys and girls from many different directions. Sometimes it is challenging to find the strength and energy to be a warm, loving, caring, and guiding parent to children. Perhaps there is a situation in the home that is troubling to us as grandparents. This is when we can pray for the parents of our grandchildren that peace and love prevail in their home. We can ask God to give parents wisdom and understanding to nurture their precious children — for them to be loving parents and good role models. And, most importantly, base their actions, reactions, and discipline on Biblical principles.

Prayers for My Grandchildren's Parents

Lord, I ask You to give my grandchildren a peaceful, faith-filled home. Give their parents much wisdom and patience in rearing them. Guide them as they make important and sometimes difficult decisions and show them:

- *how to discipline fairly*
- *how to pray effectively*
- *how to guide their children in future choices they'll need to make.*

Please help them to be impartial, kind, and loving. Since children are great imitators, I pray their parents will live a godly lifestyle worthy of imitation. Show these parents how to pray during each phase of the children's young lives. May my grandchildren's parents know the comfort of Your guidance daily.

How I thank you for the positive attributes I see in my children's parenting skills. Help me to encourage them, reinforcing their family goals and values.

Lord, when the time comes, help my grandchildren's parents be ready and willing to release their children into adulthood, free and confident to be men and women in their own right. Amen.

Lord, clothe my grandchildren's parents with strength—
Your special, extraordinary strength—as they endeavor to
be the best parents they can be.

Help my children always remember that their
children are a gift from the Lord—to be cherished,
trained, disciplined and loved.
(Psalm 127:3; Proverbs 22:6)

Lord, help my grandchildren's parents bring them up
in the nurture of the Lord. Help them not to
embitter their children lest they become discouraged.
(Ephesians 6:4; Colossians 3:21)

The Treasure Box

One grandmother, who seldom sees her grandson and grieves because he doesn't live in a Christian home, came up with a creative way to reach him. She put together a "treasure box" with small children's books about the Bible, coloring books of biblical characters, a key chain, and other small trinkets purchased at a Christian bookstore. Whenever she visits, her grandson uncovers the "treasure box" and tells her what he's learned from the Bible. Once he told her, "Sometimes I go out under the big tree in the back and read these books you sent. And I talk to God. I try to do it like you do, Grandma."

This grandmother prays every day for her little grandson and believes that he will walk in the ways of the Lord. In the meantime, she keeps asking God to show her other ways to teach him Christian principles since he's not getting instruction at home.

Prayers for Grandchildren with Unbelieving Parents

Lord, I pray for my grandchild's parents to return to the faith of their youth. Help them establish a godly home. May they have a hunger for a righteous life and not only turn their hearts toward You but also teach their own youngster the things of the Lord. In the meantime, Father, protect my grandson from ungodly influences such as harsh language and unfair treatment. Put an umbrella of Your protection and love over him. I thank you in advance for doing this. Amen.

May the time soon come when my grandchild's parents repent and turn to God so that their sins may be wiped out and times of refreshing may come to them from the Lord.
(Acts 3:19)

71

Adopted Grandchildren

Adopted children often struggle to feel accepted by
parents, siblings and members of the extended family.
Here's where a "new" grandma can prove a strong
influence—through her insightful prayers. In Ruby's case
she began to pray for a little girl, whom her son Joe
would later adopt.

When Ruby met her future daughter-in-law, Sherry and
her one-year old daughter Chris, she loved them
immediately. Soon after Chris turned two, Ruby's son Joe
married Sherry, and at the wedding ceremony they
dedicated Chris to the Lord. From the time she met this

child, Ruby and her husband
prayed everyday that Chris would
grow to "love the Lord with all her
heart and with all her soul and
with all her strength and with all
her mind" (Luke 10:27). Now other
grandchildren have been born, and
Ruby still prays faithfully for Chris
along with the others. To Grandma
Ruby there is no distinction
between them—they are all hers and she loves and prays
for them all.

Prayers for My Adopted Grandchildren

Heavenly Father, thank you for our newly adopted granddaughter. Show her parents how to care for her, making her know she is truly loved. Help them provide a strong emotional support so that she will never feel rejection or abandonment because she is adopted. May she grow up to know and honor You. I thank you for her birth parents and I ask Your blessing upon them as well.

Thank you for this new grandchild who has entered my life through adoption. May he always know he "belongs" in our family. Teach me how to pray for him all the days of his life. May I be there for him just as I am for my other grandchildren and may he feel my deep love and acceptance. Amen.

Father, we know that in all things You work for the good of those who love You, who have been called according to Your purpose. So I thank you because You knew all along what You had in store for this child when he was born.
(Romans 8:28)

Blended Families and Step-Grandchildren

Since nearly a third of all children growing up today will be part of a stepfamily before they reach adulthood, chances are some of us grandmothers will gain some step-grandchildren. Grandma Lori prays for her five step-grandchildren just as she does for her natural-born grandchildren. She finds herself praying a lot more often for God to give the family unity, unconditional love, and understanding because their blended family comes from different backgrounds and cultures.

Prayers for Step-Grandchildren's Parents and Family

Thank you for my new step-grandchildren. Show their parents how to lovingly accept each other's children and make them all feel genuinely received and loved in this blended family. When there are misunderstandings, bring understanding; when confusion, bring peace; when unfairness, bring fairness. May they all grow closer in a bond of love, knitted together by the Lord Jesus Christ.

My Father, I thank you that all of these children will be taught by the Lord, and great will be my step-grandchildren's peace; in righteousness they will be established; no weapon forged against them will prevail—this is the heritage of the servants of the Lord.
(Isaiah 54:13–14, 17)

Praying for Divorced Parents

When a family is separated through divorce, we grand-mothers must pray for all concerned, not taking sides.

Lord, I pray for both of my grandson's parents who are now divorced. May each parent rely on You to help him or her through this painful transition. I'm grateful You are in the business of restoring broken hearts and healing damaged families, and I ask first of all that you might restore this family. Give them wisdom for how to handle the problems their child will face. Cover them with Your love and safekeeping. Amen.

Lord, as these parents interact with one another and with their child may they ask You for wisdom—wisdom that comes from heaven that is pure, peace-loving, considerate, submissive, full of mercy, good fruit, impartial and sincere. Keep them from arguments and quarrels.
(James 3:17; 2 Timothy 2:23)

Single Parents

The fragmentation of families today has left many single parents struggling to raise their children alone. They need their grandmothers to back them in prayer for their own emotional wholeness as well as for God's grace to help them raise their children without the help of a spouse. A grandmother's prayerful concern can be a strong positive influence in the lives of single parents and their children.

Prayers for a Parent Raising a Child Alone

Lord, bless this parent who is raising her son alone. Help them both heal from wounds and unpleasant memories. May they look forward to the future with hope.

Lord, I thank you that You will never leave nor forsake my grandchild—nor his parent. Let them say with confidence "The Lord is my helper; I will not be afraid."
(Hebrews 13:5–6).

Prayer for Parent Separated from a Child

Ease the ache in this parent's life from the pain of not being allowed to see the children as often as he or she would like. Help him/her trust You with the children's upbringing. Show him/her ways to express love when with the children and when absent from them.

Scriptures For Meditation

The LORD is gracious and righteous;
our God is full of compassion.
The LORD protects the simplehearted;
when I was in great need, he saved me.
Psalm 116:5–6

Bear with each other and forgive whatever
grievances you may have against one another.
Forgive as the Lord forgave you.
Colossians 3:13

Be devoted to one another in brotherly love.
Honor one another above yourselves. . . . Be joyful
in hope, patient in affliction, faithful in prayer.
Romans 12:10, 12

A Grandchild's Story

Cynthia had prayed for her youngest son and his wife for years, that they would establish a Christian home and take their children to church. There was no outward sign that her prayer was answered. But when each of the two grandchildren turned four years old their parents enrolled them in a Christian pre-school. So Mickie and Michael heard Bible stories five days a week, and they learned about Jesus, the Savior.

One day Grandmother Cynthia was sitting with seven-year-old Mickie when she asked Cynthia a question with a very worried look on her face.

"Granny, can you be a Christian if you don't go to church?"

"Yes, oh, my, yes, honey," Granny Cynthia answered. "Going to church does not make someone a Christian. But having Jesus in your heart does."

A big smile lit up Mickie's little face. "Boy, I'm sure glad to hear that. Because I am one—I really am a Christian though I don't get to go to church! Granny's heart sang praise to God. "Thank you Lord. Now I'm praying with fresh hope that a little child will lead her parents to You."

Praying for Friends and Schools

A friend loves at all times. ...
   There is a friend who sticks closer than
      a brother.
Proverbs 17:17; 18:24

Our grandchildren's friends need our prayers too! Because friends will no doubt influence our grandchildren in choices they will face, we grandmothers will want to pray for the friends they already have and for those they will make in the future. Often it is at school where they meet and make close friends, so we also need to pray regularly for our grandchildren's school life—their classmates, teachers, and administrators.

We can begin now to pray for the right friends to come into our grandchildren's lives and continue praying for them through each season of their lives—from babyhood through childhood, from teen years on into adulthood.

When Donald was in high school his Grandmother Emily became greatly concerned because he was such close friends with an older boy named Shawn. She knew Donald's parents had asked him not to associate with this boy, yet they still met secretly and sometimes stayed out late to drink. Once they had a car accident. When these two got together, it always spelled big trouble!

Grandmother Emily and Donald's mom had prayed on the phone for months about everything they knew to pray, especially asking God to remove Shawn from Donald's life. After more prayer, they decided on a different prayer strategy. The two of them, mother and daughter, would pray for God's blessings on Shawn and for him to find his purpose. They prayed, too, that he would have a heart ready to allow Christ to change him. Their "blessing prayers" were offered to God on behalf of a teenager who was still trying to lead Donald astray.

This is how Grandma Emily prayed:

"God, You reversed Job's captivity when he prayed for his friends, so I choose to pray for my grandchild's friend, Shawn. Please accomplish Your will in this young man's life. May he come to know the Savior. Christ said to bless those who mistreat you—and Shawn has mistreated my grandson. But I speak blessings over him, and ask You to change his heart. Now Lord, help my grandson not be captive any longer to this young man's influence. Thank you that You love both of these boys and desire the best for them. Amen" (Job 42:10; Luke 6:27-28).

A few months later, quite unexpectedly, Shawn received a scholarship and moved to another state to study for a career in which he had great potential. Not only had God blessed Shawn, but he later came to know Christ. With Shawn no longer around, Donald developed several other good friends who had a positive effect on him. Donald soon experienced a dramatic encounter with God and after his college graduation, he went on to teach at a Christian college.

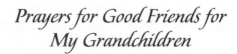

Prayers for Good Friends for My Grandchildren

Lord, bring the right friends into my grandchildren's lives—companions who will hearten, reassure, cheer, and root for them, ones who will encourage and inspire them and who will fire them up to do their best.

Father, I thank you for my grandchildren's friends who are loving and kind, providing a positive influence in their lives. Thank you that these Christian friends will help them resist temptation. Together may they learn the truth that he who walks with the wise grows wise, so that they can help each other expand in their faith and in their walk with You. I thank you that You will guide my grandchildren and their friends along godly paths. May their delight be in the law of the Lord.
(Proverbs 13:20; Psalm 1:1–2)

Father God, help my grandchildren remain strong in their convictions to do what is morally right, like Daniel and his three friends in the Bible. Strengthen my grandchildren to be good influences and resist peer pressure.
(Daniel 1:8, 12; 3:14–15)

Prayer for Jesus to Be Their Best Friend

Lord, I'm asking that Jesus be my grandchildren's best friend. May they come to know Him in an intimate way, keep His commandments, and know they can always talk to him.
(John 15:14)

Praying for My Grandchildren's Schools

It is vital that we pray for our grandchildren's schools as well as for those who teach them. One day soon after school had started, I went to pick up my five-year-old grandson Lyden Benjamin, from his public school kindergarten class. "Mama Quin, meet my teacher ..." he said, pulling on my skirt. As I shook Miss Terry's hand, I told her, "I'm glad to finally meet you. I pray for you every day since you teach one of my grandchildren."

"Thank you so much," she replied. "Lyden's mom says the two of them pray for me every morning before class. That

really blesses me, and we teachers need prayer."

Just as I made it a habit for years to pray for my children's teachers, I now pray for my grandchildren's.

Prayers for My Grandchildren's Teachers

Lord, I thank you for the teachers who will instruct my grandchildren this year.

Give them wisdom and strength, creativity and keen insight for performing their tasks. Help them know how best to help my grandchildren develop their individual skills and talents. May these teachers treat their students with patience and understanding.

Bless the teachers who will have such a profound and lasting effect on my grandchildren.

Thank you, God, that you give wisdom, knowledge and happiness to those who please you. I pray that my grandchildren's teachers will please you and that you will give them the needed attributes for teaching.
(Ecclesiastes 2:26).

Elizabeth's Hurt Feelings

Once when nine-year-old Elizabeth was preparing to say her goodnight prayers at her grandmother's home, she asked Grandma Dena to pray for her because the boys in her class were calling her "short," "small" and other names that hurt her feelings. She is in fact, a petite, blonde, blue-eyed girl with leadership qualities who serves as vice president of the third-grade class.

Several days later Grandma Dena had an insight while praying for Elizabeth. Though her grandchild was unaware of it, she equated the taunts from others who called her "little" as meaning she was "powerless." Her grandmother shared a Scripture with her from the Apostle Paul:

"Jesus said, 'My grace is sufficient for you, for my power is made perfect in weakness.' Therefore I will boast all the more gladly about my weaknesses, so that Christ's power may rest on me" (2 Corinthians 12:9).

Elizabeth nodded in understanding. Yes, she decided, the Lord's grace was sufficient for her. She chose not to let the boys' teasing upset her. She even began to smile when they called her "little" and they didn't know what to think of her reaction. But Elizabeth knew her self-esteem was intact.

Prayers for My Grandchildren's Classmates

Classmates, Lord, will play a vital role in my grandchildren's lives at school. I pray that my grandchildren will make friends with classmates who are courteous, trustworthy, honest, and helpful. May their friends also learn how to apply themselves to learn their lessons well.

Help my grandchildren and their classmates be
quick to listen in the schoolroom.
(James 1:19)

Grandma Louise watched as her first grade grandson, Lyle, struggled in his new school, complaining every day that he had to attend. She prayed about how to help him. "Go to a bookstore," the Lord seemed to impress her. Once there she carefully selected some simple books on subjects he liked—penguins, whales, stars and insects. Her aim: to show Lyle that learning could be fascinating. Wonders and mysteries of the world around him could be explored more fully as he learned to read. She kept some of the books at her home to read to him when he came to visit; others she sent home for his parents to read to him.

Whenever Grandma Louise sat on the porch at night, reading about the solar system, and pointing out interests in the sky, Lyle would reply, "I didn't know that. Read some more." Learning didn't seem so imposing when Grandma was making learning fun. Grandma Louise explained to him that treasures lay hidden in the pages of the book, but Lyle also had to learn to master math and how to write legibly as well. She watched him blossom as he began to share with his younger cousins some of the things he learned from Grandma's books. Soon he even had something to share in class. Grandma Louise continues to pray daily for him to develop more fully in the areas where he is weakest, and for him to gain self-confidence in areas of his strengths. Learning, he's discovered, is not so boring after all!

Prayers for My Grandchildren's Learning

Lord, I pray for my grandchildren to have keen ability to learn. May they show aptitude for every kind of learning, be well informed, quick to understand and qualified for what they will need to do in their studies.
(Daniel 1:4)

৶

Dear God, I am asking that the Spirit of the Lord will rest upon my grandchildren—the Spirit of wisdom and of understanding, the Spirit of counsel and of power, the Spirit of knowledge and of the fear of the Lord—for the fear of the Lord is the beginning of knowledge.
(Isaiah 11:2; Proverbs 1:7)

৶

Help my grandchildren, like Solomon, to have wisdom and great insight and breadth of understanding as measureless as the sand on the seashore.
(1 Kings 4:29)

৶

Lord, I thank you that all my grandchildren will be taught by the Lord, and great will be their peace.
(Isaiah 54:13)

৶

Scriptures for Meditation

Wisdom is more precious than rubies,
and nothing you desire can compare with her.
Proverbs 8:11

I keep asking that the God of our Lord Jesus Christ,
the glorious Father, may give you the Spirit of
wisdom and revelation, so that you may know
him better. I pray also that the eyes of your heart
may be enlightened in order that you may know the
hope to which he has called you, the riches of his
glorious inheritance in the saints, and his
incomparably great power for us who believe.
Ephesians 1:17–19

A Grandchild's Story

Great-grandmother Faye was upset when she heard her little grandson Cody using bad language and trying to live up to a "tough guy image." Friends at school called him names because he was smaller than most boys he played with, and he always seemed to want to fist fight to get back at them. She told him, "Cody, you are not mean. You are a good boy and I love you." Then she kept praying God would change him.

Through God's work in his life, Cody began to believe what his great-grandma told him and today they share a special bond. "I simply cared when others put him down," says Great-grandmother Faye. "Cody has changed so much. He excels in baseball, gets along well with others and has a sweet nature. I thank God who can do all things. I have a 'good' little great grandson now who loves Jesus."

Praying Through Health Issues

Heal me, O LORD, and I will be healed;
save me and I will be saved,
for you are the one I praise.
Jeremiah 17:14

When our grandchildren are ill, the same God who created their bodies has the power to heal them—whether our own faith is big or as small as a mustard seed. There is, of course, no guarantee that every prayer we utter for healing will result in a miracle. The point is that we put our faith in God, not in a miracle.

When my two-year-old granddaughter Victoria was hospitalized for a week with double pneumonia and wasn't responding well to treatment, I prayed continually for her recovery. Several times that week my daughter (her mom), my husband, and I stood over her hospital bed and laid our hands on her fevered brow to ask God's healing touch to come to her lungs and respiratory system.

While her parents took turns staying with Victoria her four-year-old brother slept over at my house. Several times each night we'd stop to pray together for Victoria. "Heal, Sissy, Lord Jesus, please heal my sister," he'd pray. I'd add my "amen" to his. Finally Victoria was allowed to go home. How we celebrated her restoration to health!

Prayers for My Grandchildren's Illnesses and Injuries

Lord, my grandchild is so sick. Give the doctors wisdom even beyond their experience to know how to treat her illness. Please restore her health. I praise You that You are a God of power, the Creator God who knows my grandchild so intimately. Touch her now, O gentle Savior. Amen.

Lord, Your word says if anyone is sick, he should call the church elders to pray over him. The prayer offered in faith will make the sick person well, and the Lord will raise him up. Lord, please send people with faith to pray for my sick grandchild. You say the prayers of a righteous person are effective. I praise You and trust You, Lord with this situation.
(James 5:14–16)

⌁

Lord, I know nothing is impossible for You. When Jesus lived on this earth, He went throughout the land healing every disease and sickness among the people. Your Word says Jesus Christ is the same yesterday, today and forever. So I know You still heal today. Do so for my grandchild, Lord, please heal her.
(Luke 1:37; Matthew 4:23; Hebrews 13:8)

⌁

Prayers for Good Health for My Grandchildren

Lord, help my grandchildren to acquire good health habits—to eat sensibly, to obtain proper sleep, and to get plenty of exercise and fresh air. Impress on them the importance of keeping their bodies healthy and in shape. Amen.

Thank you, Heavenly Father, for the reminder that we are God's temple and that God's Spirit lives in us. Our "temple" or body is sacred, and we are not to destroy it. May my grandchildren take good care of their bodies for their health's sake and to honor You, their Creator.
(1 Corinthians 3:16)

Jerry and Grandma Susan

Grandma Susan's grandson, Jerry, has muscular dystrophy and a life expectancy of eighteen years. She has prayed through the years for the Lord to overcome the disability, totally heal him, and give him a long and productive life. She's thankful that Jerry, who has now turned eighteen, has a great attitude. She says he talks about Jesus to anyone who is willing to have a conversation with him.

Jerry's grandparents moved from another state to be closer to him, and though it's still a two-hour drive, they travel to see him as often as possible. On these visits Jerry and his Grandmother Susan pray together, laugh, and talk about anything on Jerry's heart. On occasion they might study Bible passages on healing, health, and heaven.

Grandma Susan's Prayer for Jerry

Lord, I praise You for allowing me to have this wonderful grandchild in my life. I pray for You, O God, to lead the hands and direct the minds of the doctors and all associated with my grandson's treatment. I pray for medical breakthroughs for this disease.

I know it is not impossible for You to completely heal him, yet I trust You for Your plan for his life-span. I pray for his discomfort to subside and for him to lead as normal a life as possible. Most of all I'm grateful he has an ongoing relationship with You and will someday be with You in heaven. Give him stamina to endure and faith to trust You completely with his life.

I pray for his parents to have the strength, peace, and courage they need to continue to take care of him at home. Show those of us in his family creative ways to express Your love to Jerry. Lord, we need Your help and comfort for what lies ahead. I ask this in Jesus' name. Amen.

A Special Needs Child

When Grandma Nancy's grandson Jacob was born with
Down's Syndrome, at first she experienced denial and
pain, like the wind had been knocked out of her. When
reality moved in, she finally felt God's peace. She wrote:
"One day when Jacob was two months old, I baby-sat for
him and something very special happened when he
woke up from his nap. He smiled at me. I fed him his
bottle and he cooed and smiled again. It was like a down
payment on more to come!

Yesterday a couple in California wrote us about their
granddaughter with Down's. It was so encouraging! They
said every gift God gives is a good one and that we've
been given a very special blessing from the Lord. I could
only receive a word like that from someone who's been
there. This is a completely new path for all of us. I'm glad
God's in charge and we can lean on the Lord."

A Prayer from Grandma Nancy

Thank you Lord for this chance to trust You when I cannot understand it all. Help me keep my eyes on Jesus and His eternal view. Jacob and people like him offer us a chance to be compassionate and loving. I am trusting You, my Father, to do what's best. Accomplish Your perfect will for all involved. May my grandson come to know You at an early age and always love and praise You. Let him go beyond the limits the doctors set for him—to accomplish Your will and purpose for his life. I trust You to do this, my Savior. Amen.

Prayers for a Special Needs Child

Lord, I come to You with a grateful heart that You made each of my grandchildren different. You love our little special needs one even more than we do. Just as You created the splendor of the heavens—the sun with one kind of splendor, the moon another and the stars another—and each star differs from every other star in splendor, so You created each of Your children. I celebrate their differences and ask You to help me be a sensitive grandmother to all of them.
(1 Corinthians 15:41)

Grandmother's Prayer for Healing

Mona was expecting her first child. During a pre-natal examination, doctors found five polyps that they suspected were malignant. They advised her to terminate the pregnancy. She and her husband told the doctors straight out that they would not do that because abortion was not an option to them.

Devastated over the news, Mona asked her mom to pray, and to also call her grandparents who were living in Florida for the winter. Grandmother Vi and Granddad asked their church congregation to join them in praying for Mona's healing and for the safety of the baby in her womb.

A woman who heard the prayer request came to Grandmother Vi and said, "Let's pray that the cells that are causing this problem will be killed, just die out." Grandmother Vi and her husband prayed this daily.

Mona went for the biopsy feeling extremely hopeful. But her regular doctor was still concerned and pessimistic. He sent her to an oncologist for further examination. After that doctor had thoroughly studied the biopsy results, he was smiling when he came to give her his opinion. "These cells are all dead, or benign" he told her. "There is no problem here." *Dead cells.* That was what Mona's grandparents in Florida, and their church congregation, were praying for. What a time of joy they had in praising God for this miracle!

Little brown-eyed Kristi was born right on time, healthy. Her great-grandparents immediately began the trip in their recreational vehicle to go see this newest member of the family. Kristi's mom is doing just fine, too.

Scripture for Meditation

Praise the Lord, O my soul,
*   and forget not all his benefits—*
who forgives all your sins
*   and heals all your diseases …*
who satisfies your desires with good things
*   so that your youth is renewed like the eagle's.*
Psalm 103:2–3, 5

I pray that you may enjoy good health and that all
may go well with you, even as your soul is getting
along well.
3 John 2

"For you who revere my name, the sun of
righteousness will rise with healing in its wings,"
says the LORD.
Malachi 4:2

Sonny's Healing

Sonny crushed her ankle in an accident when she was in the fourth grade. Doctors said she'd probably never walk again. But her great-grandmother, who lived with her family, refused to give up the hope. She kept telling Sonny that she would not only walk, but would also be able to participate in the sports she loved. "She prayed," Sonny said, "asking God to restore my ankle and she never questioned it—I *would* walk. She kept encouraging me." For a year Sonny's right foot dragged and she walked with a noticeable limp. Her Nonnie kept praying. By sixth grade Sonny was running like any normal child. "My great-grandmother had something so pure about her. She never criticized people, she was always positive, and folks who wanted prayer just dropped by to visit her at our house," Sonny said. "She'd pray with great faith for their needs, just as she had prayed for me when I had a broken ankle."

Praying Through Hurts

Praise be to the God and Father of our Lord Jesus Christ, the Father of compassion and the God of all comfort, who comforts us in all our troubles, so that we can comfort those in any trouble with the comfort we ourselves have received from God.
2 Corinthians 1:3–4

When hurts assail our grandchildren, whether physical or emotional, once again a grandmother's prayers can help bring peace during confusion and hope in desperation. Hurts may vary but they are real—loneliness, disappointment, false accusation, abuse, rejection, even pain of alienation because of divorce. During these crises we grandmothers should ask God to reveal how to pray according to His will.

Lord, come in Your power
Come in Your comfort
Come in Your wisdom
Come with the balm of Gilead
To touch and heal my grandchildren's hurts.

Thank you that Jesus bore sufferings on the cross for them.

Prayer for Healing the Hurting Grandchild

Lord, I thank you for sending Jesus to bind up the brokenhearted, to comfort those who mourn and grieve, to give them beauty instead of ashes, the oil of gladness instead of mourning and a garment of praise instead of a spirit of despair. Help my grandchildren to lean into the Lord when they are hurting, and exchange their heaviness for joy.
(Isaiah 61:1–3)

Praise be to the Lord, to God our Savior, who daily bears my grandchildren's burdens.
(Psalm 68:19)

Loneliness and Disappointment

When Jennifer's family moved across country during her
senior year of high school, she cried most of the way
there, dreading the loneliness she'd face. Leaving behind
her best friends was just too much, she thought, even if
her Dad had to take the new job offer. Hurting from
disappointment, she couldn't understand why she could
not stay and finish high school where she was a popular
student. Even after she settled in her new school, she
made no effort to make friends. After school she locked
herself in her bedroom, listening to music or phoning
some of her old friends, which added to her loneliness.

One afternoon as her grandmother called to ask how
she was doing, Jennifer started sobbing and admitted
her deep loneliness and bitter disappointment.
Her grandmother promised to pray for her to make
new friends. Daily her grandmother brought this
request before the Lord.

Three months later Jennifer had become acquainted with
two classmates who were going off to the same college
she had chosen. Together they looked forward to
developing their friendships further as they planned for
their fall semester.

Prayer for My Grandchild's Loneliness

Lord, heal my grandchild's sense of loneliness. Bring someone into her life to encourage her and give her hope. Help her to reach out to be a friend first of all, then she will have a friend. Thank you that You will comfort

her and heal her broken heart. Bring friends of Your choice across her path. I thank you in advance for doing this. Amen.

*Lord, please turn to my grandchild
and be gracious to her, for she is
lonely and the troubles of her heart
have multiplied. Look upon her in
distress and move by Your mighty
power to heal her.*
(Psalm 25:16–18)

Prayers for My Disappointed Grandchild

Lord, my grandchild is struggling through big disappointments—disappointment in herself, disappointment in the person who let her down, disappointment in expectations that didn't materialize. Give her hope that You have a solution bigger than her disappointment. Help her emerge from this temporary setback stronger than ever in her faith, confident that You will never leave her nor forsake her.

May the God of hope fill my grandchild with joy and peace as he trusts in You, so that he may overflow with hope by the power of the Holy Spirit.
(Romans 15:13)

During their disappointments, teach my grandchildren how to be strong and take heart, and wait for the Lord.
(Psalm 27:14)

O God, may this verse be in their hearts as they walk through tough disappointments:

Praise be to the LORD, for he has heard my cry for mercy. The LORD is my strength and my shield, my heart trusts in him, and I am helped. My heart leaps for joy and I will give thanks to him in song.
(Psalm 28:6–7)

Praying Through My Grandchild's Fears

Fears will no doubt attempt to snare our grandchildren sometime during their growing up years. They may loom large as fear of failure, fear of ridicule, fear of losing a relationship, fear of injury or disease, fear of losing a loved one, or even fear of the future. Fear coupled with worry can become a giant obstacle to our grandchildren—and very real. Again, we grandmothers can help ward off this arrow of hurt with our prayers.

Let my grandchildren be so enmeshed in Your love Lord, that no fear can overcome them. Help them put their trust and faith in You, knowing You are able to deliver them from any fear.

When my grandchildren are afraid, help them trust in You.
Yes, let them say, "In God I trust; I will not be afraid.
What can mortal man do to me?"
(Psalm 56:3–4)

Keep my grandchildren from being anxious about any-
thing, but in everything, by prayer and petition, with
thanksgiving may they present their requests to God. And
the peace of God which transcends all understanding will
guard their hearts and minds in Christ Jesus.
(Philippians 4:6–7)

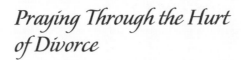

Praying Through the Hurt of Divorce

Divorce and its aftermath are terribly traumatic for children, and grandmothers should pray faithfully for those hurting from the broken home. While worries about their future loom larger than life, some children of divorce may have a hard time communicating honestly with their parents—expressing their deep emotions and hurts. A grandmother can be there for them, letting them know whatever they want to say to her is all right.

We can ask God to make us sensitive listeners as well as wise counselors when our grandchildren come to us for advice or guidance. Most of all, we can let them know we will always be there for them, believing in them and praying for them through their hurts and disappointments.

A Grandchild's Story

When Grandma Flo's son and his wife divorced, she grieved as she watched three of their four children take up offenses against their mom. The gall of bitterness was eating at their emotions, especially after the explosive court proceedings. It bothered her terribly that the twenty-three year-old daughter, especially, held such deep grudges, even admitting she hated her own mom. While Grandma Flo prayed many Scriptures for her grandchildren, she especially personalized a passage from Proverbs.

Flo prayed, "Lord, help my grandchildren pay attention and listen closely to Your words; help them to keep those words in their hearts, for they are life to those who find them, and health to a man's whole body. Help them to guard their hearts for they are the wellspring of life. Enable them to put away perversity from their mouths and keep corrupt talk from their lips. Help them to let their eyes look straight ahead, fixing their gaze directly on You. Make level paths for their feet and let them take only ways that are firm. Help them not to swerve to the right or the left; but keep their feet from evil" (Proverbs 4:20–27).

Flo also prayed that her grandchildren would realize their need to forgive their parents and would come to a place where they could express genuine love to them.

She prayed, "Lord, the Bible says when we pray, if we hold anything against anyone, we must forgive so that our Father in heaven may forgive us our sins. Please help my grandchildren make that decision so they will no longer be in bondage to their unforgiveness and hurts" (Mark 11:25).

Prayers for a Grandchild Hurt Through Divorce

Lord, my heart aches for my grandchild since his parents' divorce. Keep his parents from wounding him further. Help them not to take out their own anger and frustrations on their son. Guard his heart and his emotions. Help him understand that the divorce is not his fault and that he can still show love to both his parents.

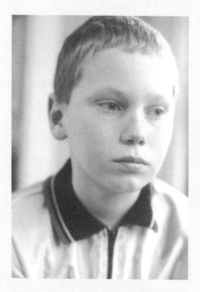

Bring healing to his heart. When he does feel abandoned, help him deal appropriately with his anger. Keep him from fear of the future as he learns to rely more and more on You. Show him how much he is loved—beyond measure by his parents, his Heavenly Father, and by me, his always-praying Grandma. Amen.

*Lord, I ask that my granddaughter will not fear
the future, for You are with her. Keep her from
being dismayed, for You are her God. You will
strengthen her and help her. You will uphold her
with your righteous right hand.*
(Isaiah 41:10)

⁓

*During the different stages of his life when
my grandson needs godly male examples, please,
Lord, bring friends, mentors, and teachers who
will help him in his Christian walk.
When my granddaughter needs a godly
woman—one with a listening ear and wise
counsel to advise her—please, Lord, bring the
one of Your choice into her life. Lord, may those
mentors in speech, conduct, love, faith, and
purity, show themselves as an example of those
who believe. Help them use the spiritual gifts
within them as they exhort and teach my
grandchildren.*
(1 Timothy 4:12,14, NASB)

⁓

Praying When a Loved One Dies

Many children are not able to express their hurt or fears when someone close to them dies. Grandmoms can pray with a child through every phase of the grieving process. Holding the grieving child close to you and allowing him a shoulder to cry on will often help ease his own sense of loss. Letting him talk with someone who has also been through a similar loss and has attained acceptance without bitterness is another option. Grieving will take time.

Reminiscing about the loved one he lost, or even pouring over pictures together may help as an outlet for grief. The other day I was telling two of my small grandchildren about my mother who died before they were born. I explained how she is in heaven now, but she prayed many prayers for them even though she didn't know their names. Six-year-old Benjamin said to me, "I'll always remember you, Mama Quin — even after you are dead and gone. And, I won't forget you prayed for me every day, either."

We can pray that our grandchildren will not feel abandoned,
or take blame for the death of a
loved one. As grandmothers, we
can help in the recovery process
by providing listening ears.

Grandparents can help the
younger generation see mortality
for what it is, and the promise of
life after death for those who know the Savior. We can
pray, asking Christ to ease the pain and provide healing
and comfort for the brokenhearted. We can also ask God
to help us find creative ways to offer unconditional love
and comfort during this painful period in our
grandchildren's lives.

Prayer for a Grandchild Who is Grieving the Loss of a Loved One

Lord, help my grandchild cope with the death of her (friend, parent, sibling). Fill the void she feels with Your love. Comfort and strengthen her. Keep her from guilt and

from blaming herself or You. Help her remember the good times they enjoyed together. Thank you for the hope of eternal life with You. As my grandchild works through her grief, let her know she must go on living. Bring her through to healing of her hurt over this devastating loss. I thank you for being her Comforter. In Jesus' name. Amen.

Lord, as she walks through the grief of "the valley of the shadow of death" over losing a loved one let my grandchild fear no evil, for You are with her. You comfort her.
(Psalm 23:4)

~

Dear God, I thank you that You so loved the world that You gave Your one and only Son, so that whoever believes in Him shall not perish but have eternal life. Thank you that my grandchild knows her loved one is in heaven because he chose Your salvation promise.
(John 3:16)

~

Scriptures for Meditation

*I saw the Holy City, the new Jerusalem,
coming down out of heaven from God,
prepared as a bride beautifully dressed
for her husband. And I heard a loud voice
from the throne saying, "Now the dwelling
of God is with men, and he will live with them.
They will be his people, and God himself
will be with them and be their God and
He will wipe every tear from their eyes.
There will be no more death, or mourning
or crying or pain, for the old order of
things has passed away."*
Revelation 21:2–4

A Grandchild's Story

As soon as Grandma Portia heard that her eight-year-old granddaughter Sandy had been viciously attacked by two dogs, she prayed continuously as she sped to the hospital to be with her.

"Lord, please come in Your power, with Your healing, and touch my granddaughter. I pray that she will not be badly scarred. Keep fear from invading her soul because of this traumatic experience." Grandma Portia knew that Sandy could be physically crippled, as well as emotionally wounded, if fear followed her all her life.

At the emergency room, doctors painted the worst picture imaginable because Grandma Portia was a nurse and could understand their medical jargon. However, she believed her God was her granddaughter's healer, and one day Sandy would walk and would not be permanently maimed. While speaking words of encouragement to Sandy, Grandma Portia would stop every now and then and pray aloud right at her hospital bed.

Finally, after several successful surgeries, Sandy was able to walk normally and had only minimal scar tissue on her leg and arm. Today she is a teenager, and miracle of all, she has absolutely no fear of dogs—just as her grandmother had prayed.

Praying for *Wayward Grandchildren*

The LORD will fulfill his purpose for me;
your love, O LORD, endures forever—
do not abandon the works of your hands.
Psalm 138:8

We grandmothers must never, ever give up on a grandchild who seems to be wandering in a wilderness of his own making. When our grandchild turns away from God, how heartbreaking it is for those who wait for his return. Years may tick by before that grandchild makes an "about face" and starts toward home. Here is one grandmother's story:

Grandmother Joan began praying for her grandson, Steven, from the moment of his birth and continued through some turbulent years when he ran with the wrong crowd and fell into a life of drug addiction and crime. After his parents divorced, he was raised by his alcoholic mother and stepfather. When he was jailed at nineteen on his first drug possession charge, Joan prayed harder than ever that he would come to his senses and make a turnaround.

How ironic that the day he was arrested was the day he made his comeback to the Lord. He spent the whole night praying. "Jesus had gotten my attention and I could no longer run. He not only came back into my heart, but He gave me peace that I had never known before. I knew I wasn't playing games with God anymore," he wrote to his grandmother.

Steven was sentenced to two years in prison. While serving time he shared with other inmates how God could change their lives, too. His grandmother was able to supply him with Bibles, books, tapes, and videos to help him in his study of God's word.

After his release from prison, Steven went to live with Joan and her husband, his loving, praying grandparents. Steven plans to study music so he can lead others in worshipping God. His grandmother prayed persistently for twenty-eight years for this grandson on whom she would not give up.

Prayers for Wayward Grandchildren

Lord, I'm asking You to fulfill Your purpose in my disobedient grandchild's life. I cry out for him. How I thank you that You will not abandon the work of Your hands—this precious one who once knew You so well. Bring to his remembrance the things of God that he learned as a child. I stand in the prayer gap and ask You to call him back from the land of the enemy. Give him a strong desire to live a life worthy of his potential.

Lord, open my grandchild's eyes so that she may turn from darkness to light and from the power of Satan to God, so that she may receive forgiveness of her sins, and a place among those who are sanctified by faith in Christ.
(Acts 26:18)

Grandma Intercessors Do Battle

As intercessors for our grandchildren, we come before God beseeching Him on their behalf. Other times, however, we find ourselves fighting the Adversary, saying *no* to his tactics to harass and tempt them. The Scriptures are our arsenal, our prayer manual, and our book of promises on which we stand in faith.

Prayers for the Battle

Heavenly Father, help my grandchildren to be strong in the Lord, and in His mighty power. May they continue to put on the full armor of God, so that they can take their stand against the devil's schemes. For their struggle is not against flesh and blood, but against the rulers, against the authorities, against the powers of this dark world and against the spiritual forces of evil in the heavenly realms.
(Ephesians 6:10–12)

Our Father in heaven, Your kingdom come, Your will be done in my grandchild's life; lead him not into temptation but deliver him from the evil one.
(Matthew 6:9–10,13)

A Grandma Who Won't Give Up

Grandmother Marlene has prayed for her granddaughter, Kim, for all of Kim's life. Once while visiting her grandmother when she was young, Kim prayed to receive Christ into her life. She had loved the things of God then.

But after she graduated from college, Kim's life seemed to spiral downhill. Her credit card debt was phenomenal, and she was addicted to heroin. Finally at her parents' insistence, Kim entered a drug rehabilitation program, but it just wasn't working satisfactorily because they gave her methadone, which she despised.

Grandmother Marlene enlisted several close Christian friends to agree with her in prayer that Kim would get completely free of drug addiction and once again serve the Lord.

"God in His mercy delivered her from the drugs," Grandmother Marlene said. "God is so faithful, He will never let her go. She said I'm her most favorite person in the whole world. I know she sees the love of Jesus in our home, and He is knocking at the door of her heart. She is working and she calls me collect every week so we can talk."

The following is a prayer Marlene prayed for Kim. It is from a passage in Psalms and Marlene substituted her granddaughter's name to make it personal:

"Teach Kim, O Lord, to follow your decrees;
give her understanding; help her to keep your law
and obey it with all her heart. Direct her in the
path of your commands for there she will find delight.
Turn Kim's heart toward your statutes and not toward
selfish gain. Turn her eyes away from worthless things;
preserve her life according to your word. Take away
the disgrace for your laws are good."
(Psalm 119:33–39)

Help my grandchild to cry to the Lord in her trouble, and save her from her distress. Bring my grandchild out of darkness, and the deepest gloom, and break away her chains.
(Psalm 107:13–14)

How grateful I am, Lord, because of Your great love, we are not consumed. Your compassions never fail. They are new every morning; great is Your faithfulness to my family—my grandchildren in particular. Thank you for Your continuing compassions poured out upon them. Amen.
(Lamentations 3:22–23)

Prayers to Guard My Grandchildren Against Unwholesome Influences

Lord, open my grandchild's eyes to see that the advice he is getting is foolishness. Bring to light the things hidden in the darkness and disclose the motives of men's hearts. Then show my grandchild the right choices to make.
(2 Samuel 15:31; 1 Corinthians 4:5)

⌐

Contend, O Lord, with those who contend with my grandchild. Let not his enemies gloat over him or speak false accusations. Lord, keep my grandchild from the traps set for him by evildoers.
(Psalm 35:1, 19–20; 141:9)

⌐

Keep my grandchild, O Lord from the hands of the wicked; protect him from men of violence who plan to trip his feet. You are his God! O Sovereign Lord, his strong deliverer, who shields him in the day of battle.
(Psalm 140:4, 7)

⌐

The Lost Son

There was a man who had two sons. The younger one
said to his father, "Father, give me my share of the estate."
So he divided his property between them.

Not long after that, the younger son got together all he
had, set off for a distant country and there squandered his
wealth in wild living. After he had spent everything, . . . he
began to be in need. So he went and hired himself out to
a citizen of that country, who sent him to his fields to
feed pigs. He longed to fill his stomach with the pods that
the pigs were eating, but no one gave him anything.

When he came to his senses, he said, "How many of my
father's hired men have food to spare, and here I am
starving to death! I will set out and go back to my father."
. . . So he got up and went to his father.

While he was still a long way off, his father saw him and
was filled with compassion for him; he ran to his son,
threw his arms around him and kissed him. . . .

The father said to his servants, "Quick! Bring the best
robe and put it on him. ... Bring the fattened calf and kill
it. Let's have a feast and celebrate. For this son of mine
was dead and is alive again; he was lost and is found."
So they began to celebrate.

Luke 15:11–18, 20, 22-24

A Grandchild's Story

"Jesus, where are you?" four-year old Brady ran through his grandmother's house shouting. Seems his cousin had hidden the baby Jesus that belonged in the Christmas nativity scene.

"Jesus, where are you? Come back. Come back to our house to stay," the little one kept calling as he ran from room to room looking for the lost, but very necessary, carved olive wood character that belonged in the crèche.

The missing baby Jesus, Brady knew, was only a representative of the real Jesus in heaven. But little Brady also knew that Jesus was the most important person in this scene portraying the first Christmas.

His grandmother was thrilled that her grandson wanted Jesus to come back to *her house* to stay!

As she hugged him, she prayed he would always want Jesus to be with him, keeping him close to His heart, keeping him from evil and temptation.

Praying for Financial Provision

God will meet all your needs according to his glorious riches in Christ Jesus.
Philippians 4:19

God can provide for our grandchildren when it comes to financial needs. Our prayers may be the very thing that helps prevent catastrophes and change circumstances. When we pray for financial blessings, we can also pray that our grandchildren learn to handle money wisely and that they maintain grateful and generous hearts.

As our grandchildren grow up, financial choices will challenge them and their parents—such as entering the job market right out of high school, choosing between vocational school or college, or getting more advanced instruction.

One grandmother said, "I had nothing financially to give my grandchildren, but I could and did pray for them often and with persistence. We saw God provide for them in ways we could never have imagined with scholarships, part-time jobs, reasonable housing, and favor in the marketplace," she said.

A Grandchild's Story

Grandma Gerry began praying for her grandson Gene in high school and continued to pray for Gene's spiritual condition after graduation, urging him to give His life to Christ. After he married, she also prayed for his wife Ronnie to know the Lord. In kind and loving ways she told them about God's blessings and their need to follow Him.

Gene opened his own sewing machine shop, but his business was not going well. His grandmother again urged him to trust God with his life and business, and continued to pray for them. Finally, they made the decision to commit their lives to Christ and started going to church where they became active participants. Today

Gene's business has prospered so much he has hired several employees and has plans to expand his business. One day Ronnie wrote to tell her husband's grandmother how much she appreciated her insistence that they give their lives and business to the Lord. It was the smartest move they ever made, she said.

Prayers for Financial Blessings for My Grandchildren

Lord, bless my grandchildren in the area of finances. Help them be good money managers. I pray that materialism will not become a snare to my grandchildren. Lord, give them wisdom to get and keep their finances in order. Help them not to fall into the trap of debt, buying worldly things they cannot afford. May they follow biblical principles of finances and be faithful in their tithes and offerings. Amen.

Help my grandchildren discern the difference between wants and needs and always remember that You will supply their needs according to Your glorious riches in Christ Jesus. Help them remember that a man's life does not consist in the abundance of his possessions. Help them know contentment in what they do have, maintaining grateful hearts to praise and thank You for every provision they have.
(Luke 12:15; Philippians 4:11, 19)

I praise You, O Lord, for You are my grandchild's Shepherd and he will not want. I pray he will continually praise You with a grateful heart and not forget all Your benefits to him, nor all the ways You have provided for him.
(Psalm 23:1; Psalm 103:2)

Lord, help my grandchildren to do good and to share with others, for with such sacrifices God is pleased. Lord, may my grandchildren honor You with their giving—sharing with the poor— for you bless a generous man or woman.
(Hebrews 13:16; Proverbs 22:9)

Help them be rich in good deeds, generous and willing to share, and in this way lay up treasures for themselves as a firm foundation for the coming age.
(1 Timothy 6:18–19)

Lord, I pray that my grandchildren will always seek first Your kingdom and Your righteousness.
(Matthew 6:33)

Scriptures for Meditation

The LORD bestows favor and honor;
no good thing does he withhold
from those whose walk is blameless.

Psalm 84: 11

⸎

Give, and it will be given to you. A good measure,
pressed down, shaken together and running over,
will be poured into your lap. For with the measure
you use, it will be measured to you.

Luke 6:38

⸎

I have learned the secret of being content in any and
every situation, whether well fed or hungry, whether
living in plenty or in want. I can do everything through
Christ who gives me strength.

Philippians 4:12–13

⸎

Humility and the fear of the LORD
bring wealth and honor and life.

Proverbs 22:4

⸎

Sonya's Piano

When she turned ten, Sonya desperately wanted to take
piano lessons, but she had no piano. She and her grandmother decided to pray together, believing that God
would somehow supply a piano. Several months passed.
Then one day her grandmother was at a birthday party
for a friend. Over cake and punch, she told the women
seated around her how much her granddaughter wanted
a piano. A lady sitting in the chair beside her whom she
didn't even know said, "We are getting a grand piano
since we've moved into a bigger place. I'd be glad to loan
your granddaughter our upright piano until we decide
what we want to do with it."

Three years later Sonya still has that wonderful "loan" in
her living room and she is becoming quite a good pianist.
She believes God chose the right moment to have her
grandmother mention her need to a stranger. As a result,
they saw the power of their prayer agreement: Sonya's
heart's *desire* and *need* for a lovely piano.

Sonya and her grandmother
also prayed for money to cover
the cost of Sonya's piano lessons.
Soon thereafter, her dad got a slight
monthly raise and promised it to his daughter
for her lessons.

Today the teenager still prays with her grandmother for
special things she needs as she plans for her future
schooling to become a teacher.

Praying for Future Decisions

*May God give you the desire of your heart
and make all your plans succeed.*
Psalm 20:4

While grandchildren are quite young, many grandmas begin
to pray about their developing personalities, financial stability,
future spouses, choices of friends, college, and even their career
decisions. It's never too early to begin to pray about your
grandchildren's futures.

One grandma says, "When I'm with my grandchildren,
I pray about what is important to them at the moment. But daily
I also pray *waiting prayers* for their futures. These are prayers
that I plant as seeds, and so we may wait years before the answers
come. Just as a good gardener doesn't dig up the seeds to see
how they are growing, I must leave those prayers planted. But
I continually water them with more prayers and promises from
God's Word until the grandchildren are older and face serious
life choices."

Prayers for the Future Decisions
of My Grandchildren

Lord, I pray that my grandchildren will make wise decisions in every aspect of their lives so they will excel and mature into godly men and women. Begin to reveal to them Your plan for their lives, and help them live up to their full potential. May they bring honor to You in all they do.

Lord, I thank You that Your word and Your purpose for my grandchildren will be accomplished both now and in the future. You say Your word will not return to You empty, but will accomplish what You desire.
(Isaiah 55:11)

Lord, help me stand in prayer for all my grandchildren and for their future choices. Help me not to look so much at the circumstances around them, but to believe with faith what Your Word says they can become. Thank you for the promise that You reach out and touch our offspring's offspring, generation after generation. I pray they will have a positive influence in an ungodly world—revealing Christ's love to their fellow students, neighbors, or colleagues at work.
(Deuteronomy 7:9)

A Grandchild's Story

Tony's maternal Grandmother Laura had prayed diligently for his college and future career ever since he was small. Tony loved music and he desperately wanted a musical profession. But he had been in college almost five years studying engineering because that's what his dad insisted he must do.

Tony was turning twenty-one that summer and studying hard for his engineering exams. Grandmother Laura sent a box of homemade cookies with a note of encouragement during his final week, as she always did. This time she sent a Scripture in the box, too:

"For I know the plans I have for you," declares the LORD, "plans to prosper you and not to harm you, plans to give you hope and a future. Then you will call upon me and come and pray to me, and I will listen to you. You will seek me and find me when you seek me with all your heart. I will be found by you," declares the LORD, "and will bring you back from captivity" (Jeremiah 29:11–14).

Several phrases in that verse seemed to leap into Tony's heart: *"plans to give you hope and a future ... bring you back from captivity."* His grandmother's note with the Scripture became his "turning around" point, providing him hope in his despair. He felt God was encouraging him to use his musical talents—after all He, the Creator, had given him those gifts. Soon after, Tony dropped engineering, got a full time job to pay his tuition, and enrolled in a nearby university to study music. His grandmother hasn't stopped praying for him to achieve his goals.

Prayers for the Education and Career Decisions of My Grandchildren

Lord, help each of my grandchildren to choose the right course of education for their individual talents. I pray they will prepare and follow careers that:

- *will make them happy*
- *will provide financial security*
- *will use their abilities and skills to the best advantage*
- *will enable them to make positive contributions to their neighborhoods and communities*
- *will be pleasing to You.*

O Lord, help my grandchildren to make these important and critical decisions that will influence the rest of their lives. Help them choose the right colleges and enable them to find financial plans to get them through. May my grandchildren seize every educational advantage while at college, from the right classes to the right friends to the right part-time jobs. I ask You to give them strength and endurance and the desire to diligently apply themselves. Help them come out of college better equipped to use their God-given talents.

Lord, not all of my grandchildren are cut out for college. So help them get the right training they need—whether it's through a vocational school or on-the-job training. Bring the right people to counsel them, guide them, encourage them, and mentor them along the way. Help them develop work standards that are pleasing to You. Give them happy and productive lives doing the things that make them contented. Amen.

May God's Spirit direct my grandchildren's decisions while they choose the right college or career. And may His Spirit continue to guide them all the days of their lives, giving them the needed wisdom, understanding, counsel and knowledge for what lies ahead.
(Isaiah 11:2)

Lord, when my grandchildren lack wisdom for the work ahead, let them stop and ask You, for You give generously to those who ask. Help them to believe and not doubt when they hear from You.
(James 1:5–6)

Lord, I pray that when my grandchildren feel confused, they will remember and understand that You are not a God of disorder but of peace. So let them lean into Your understanding. I ask in Jesus' name. Amen.
(1 Corinthians 14:33)

Praying for My Grandchildren's Spouses

Even when grandchildren are little, grandmas can begin to pray for the spouses their grandchildren will have someday.

Barbara was visiting in her son's home when her oldest grandson, eighteen-year-old Stephen, came into the kitchen and gave her a big hug. As they hugged, she said, "Stephen, could I pray for you? I believe God wants to release a blessing into your life from your grandmother."

"Sure, Gram," he said.

Barbara prayed for God's divine purpose and blessing upon his life, and then she prayed over the college he was planning to attend the next year. When she began to pray about his choice of a wife, and thanking God for her, Stephen chuckled.

Later Stephen wrote me about his grandmother. "I always have the comfort of knowing Gram is blanketing me with prayers, and that God is watching over my life. I've been able to stay out of trouble because of her prayers and the Lord's intervention in my life. I thank God for her every day." What a tribute to a praying grandmother.

Ten-year-old Julian wrote about how he appreciates his grandmother's prayers. "My grandma tells me she has prayed for me every day of my life and even before I was born. I'm glad she's always praying for me, even if she doesn't always know what I am doing. I understand God better because she explains things to me. Grandma prayed for her son—my dad—to get the right wife starting when he was only two years old. Now I have a loving, caring mom. Grandma says she has prayed for the right wife for me, too. I wonder what she'll be like."

Prayers for Future Mates for My Grandchildren

Lord, I ask You for divine appointments for my grandchildren to meet their future mates. I pray that You will place them in rightful positions to receive Your guidance and purpose. May each of them walk closely with God.

Lord, bring the right partner into my grandson's life at the right time. May she love the Lord God with all her heart, soul, mind and strength. May she embrace Jesus as her personal Savior and Lord. May she love my grandson with an undying love as long as they both shall live, and be a helper suitable for him. May she be rich in good deeds, generous, willing to share, and one who practices hospitality.
(Mark 12:30; Romans 10:9; Genesis 2:18; 1 Timothy 6:18; Romans 12:13)

*Lord, may my granddaughter's future husband love God
and embrace Jesus as his Savior. Help him love his wife
with a faithful love for as long as they both shall live. May
he be healthy, able to work and support a family. Help him
be a good money manager. May he and my granddaughter
establish their home with God's prescribed order as
outlined in Ephesians 5:21–28. May the two of them
be of one mind, living in peace. And may the God of love
and peace be with them. Lord, bring this partner into my
granddaughter's life in Your perfect timing.*
(2 Corinthians 13:11)

Praying for My Grandchildren's Employment

Before we know it, our grandchildren will need jobs.
Finding the right ones to match their skills may not
always be easy.

Lord, my grandchild is looking for the right job. Please
open a door of opportunity soon. Help him through the
application process and provide favor in the interview.
Match his talents with the company that needs his skills.
Thank you, Lord, for Your provision of a job for him.
Nothing is impossible for You.

May the favor of the Lord our God
rest upon my grandchildren;
establish the work of their hands for them—
yes, establish the work of their hands.
(Psalm 90:17)

Help my grandchildren remember that
whatever they do, they should work at it with
all their hearts, as working for the Lord, for it
is the Lord Christ they are serving.
(Colossians 3:23–24)

Scriptures for Meditation

Know ... that wisdom is sweet to your soul;
if you find it, there is a future hope for you,
and your hope will not be cut off.
Proverbs 24:14

"Call to me and I will answer you and
tell you great and unsearchable things you do
not know," says the Lord.
Jeremiah 33:3

"I will surely bless you and make your descendants
as numerous as the stars in the sky and as the sand
on the seashore. ... Through your offspring all
nations on earth will be blessed, because you
have obeyed me," says the Lord.
Genesis 22:17–18

Special Ways to Pray Effectively for Your Grandchildren

> *The Spirit helps us in our weakness. We do not know what we ought to pray for, but the Spirit himself intercedes for us with groans that words cannot express.*
>
> **Romans 8:26**

God's word is full of creative ways to pray both practical and Bible-based prayers. Because our personalities differ—as do those of our grandchildren—we can find a variety of "best" ways to pray that are comfortable to us, and that are also a perfect fit for the grandchildren on our hearts.

One Scripture For All Her Grandchildren

Grandmother Joyce found one Scripture she prays consistently each day for her four grandchildren. She discovered it soon after the arrival of her first grandchild when she asked God to help him grow up in the likeness of Jesus. In thinking about how Jesus grew, this Scripture came to her mind:"And

Jesus grew in wisdom and stature, and in favor with God and men" (Luke 2:52).

"I realized so many Christ-like attributes were revealed in this verse," she said."It contains a wealth of desirable traits, so I wrote my precious grandson's name beside this verse in my Bible and began to pray it daily for him. Now I have four grandchildren.Through the years this has been my most consistent prayer for them, with God showing me its application to specific circumstances and needs in their lives."

As Grandma Joyce prayed through the years, she listed requests generated by this Scripture that her grandchildren might:

Increase in wisdom by:

- *Leaning not on their own understanding*
- *Reading God's Word and memorizing Scriptures*
- *Gaining a gift of discernment*
- *Abhorring evil and clinging to good*
- *Making wise choices daily*
- *Seeking first the Kingdom of God*

Increase in stature by:

- *Seeking God's protection and provision*
- *Learning to eat healthy and exercise properly*
- *Determining to never abuse their bodies with drugs or alcohol*
- *Recognizing God as helper and healer*

Increase in favor with God by:

- *Developing a personal relationship with Him at an early age*
- *Seeking Him with all their hearts*
- *Obeying God's commands*
- *Having a love for those who are lost without the Savior*
- *Exhibiting the fruit of the Spirit*

Increase in favor with men by:

- *Obeying their parents*
- *Respecting authority*
- *Developing a positive, encouraging personality*
- *Expressing compassion for the hurting*
- *Treating others as they want to be treated*
- *Displaying God's love to those whose paths they cross*

This Scripture, she felt, covered about everything she needed to pray for her grandchildren during their spiritual development and for their future choices.

A Grandmother of Ten Tells How She Prays

For the little ones I pray about their personality.
For the grade-school-age children, I pray for their character and values.
For the teenagers, I pray about their future career and future mate.
For the adults, I pray about their home life, their walk with the Lord and their outreach to others.

Lord, I thank You for the opportunity to plant prayers for my grandchildren's future. May You answer my prayers for them in Your timing and in Your best way. Be with my grandchildren and their children after them, seeing them through hard times as well as good ones. I pray that they too will leave footprints of faith for their children and their children's children to follow. Thank you, Lord, for Your great love toward us. Amen.

What Is Prayer?

Effective praying is prayer that is in agreement with God's Word and is led by the Holy Spirit. Jesus promised, "If two of you on earth agree about anything you ask for, it will be done for you by my Father in heaven. For where two or three come together in my name, there am I with them" (Matthew 18:19–20).

Sometimes grandmothers find it helpful to pray with someone else when praying for their grandchildren. Maybe it will be a granddad, another grandmother, or even the grandchildren's parents. The force of our prayer seems to intensify when we have a prayer partner agreeing with us. Also we are greatly strengthened in our own faith in this way.

Ask God's Spirit to guide you in your prayers. Paul admonished Christians to, "Pray in the Spirit on all occasions, with all kinds of prayers and requests. With this in mind, be alert and always keep on praying for all the saints" (Ephesians 6:18).

God rewards those who earnestly seek him.
Hebrews 11:6

As grandmothers we can pass on to our children and grandchildren the greatest heritage possible—the example of our personal prayer lives after which they can model their own. Whenever opportunities come we can look for ways to talk to them about God's plan for their future. Only God knows what the results will be if we are truly faithful praying for our grandchildren, leaving them footprints of faith to follow.

When we asked women to share something about what their grandmothers' prayers have meant to them, we got many beautiful letters. My hope is that these tributes will encourage and inspire you as you continue to pray for your own grandchildren. One day you will receive the reward for your efforts when your grandchildren "rise up and call you blessed" for the prayers that you have poured into their lives.

Grandma MeeMee was petite but strong and spiritual. I loved her so much. She was always so gentle and kind to me. I loved to hear her sing her Finnish hymns in her beautiful soprano voice. She had a large Bible which sat out on the dining table when she wasn't reading from it—but she read from it a lot. And I read from her life and learned much about the Christian faith. She was always swift to let me know right from wrong. I always felt the warmth of her love, as there was a godliness about her. I often walked, picked cherries, or apples, or just sat with her, listening closely to the stories she told. I loved her pancakes with blueberry topping and I'm still hooked on them.

My Grammie was a woman of character, faith and determination. When her husband died at an early age leaving her with a daughter at home and one in college, she learned to drive, put herself through college and taught second grade until her retirement. She possessed that same "no quit" attitude with the Lord's work. I watched her teach Sunday school even at the age of eighty after suffering a stroke. After her second stroke, she lost her vision, but she kept on crocheting afghans for all of her grandchildren and great-grandchildren. Her legacy speaks volumes to me and has helped mold me into a woman of faith with the same "no quit" determination as my Grammie.

My grandmother imparted many images to me. I remember a woman who knew hard work and few luxuries; a storm cellar full of her canned foods; fruit seeds laid open drying in the sun. I remember her most, though, each time I see and handle the big, black book where she wrote about life—births, marriages and deaths—The Holy Bible.

Granny was my hero. She always remembered my birthday and other special moments in my life. But most of all, she prayed for me.

My grandmother left us a spiritual heritage. While our mother worked, Granny laid her life aside to take care of us and she loved us unconditionally—five children in all. She lived with us most of her life and she was a very humble, praying woman.

My grandmother's house was a place I loved to go because I knew she would totally accept me just as I was. She had an awe and reverence for God and all His creation that she passed on to me.

From a letter to her husband's grandmother: "You entered my life at a time when I was lost and you helped me find myself by just finding and following God. You brought me to the Lord. What a gift that has been."

After our parents divorced, my brother and I lived with Nana until we left for college. Nana provided a loving home for us and trained us in the way she thought we should go. Every morning she would pull back the kitchen curtain to welcome the day. I always heard her say, "Father, I stretch my hand to You, no other help I know. If Thou withdraw Thyself from me, Lord, where would I go?"

Nana was widowed twice by the time she was in her early thirties and she had six children of her own to raise before she took over the care of my brother and me. She was an inspiration to me as I pursued my college studies, often on scholarships she helped pray for me to get. She still lives on in me and in my children, as I've tried to pass on to my sons the love of God, the love of people, and the many pearls of wisdom that she gave me.

Prayer was as natural as breathing for my grandma. She often took my cousins and me on long walks in the woods and wading in a little creek. I'll never forget how special it was to kneel outside beside the creek with the breeze in our faces, as Grandma taught her grandchildren how to pray. What a wonderful heritage.

My Granny left me a journal of her prayers she started when I was a baby. The handwriting is faded, but I can still read the flowery phrases that tell of her trust in the Lord to help me and guide me and bless me throughout my life.

My grandmother read my favorite stories to me over and over, then I'd let her read me her favorite ones from her well-worn Bible.

My grandmother knew a lot about praise and worship and touching heaven's throne, and she imparted that to me when I was a child when she gave me my first rhythm band instruments to play. She was always humming praise songs. I know that my grandmother is in heaven cheering all of us on to finish the race on earth and bring glory to the Lord. She also modeled the gift of hospitality to me by always having a crowd around her table. Today, that gift has been passed on to the fourth generation as I try to foster these qualities in my own children.

Grandmas are fond of giving gifts to their grandchildren, but the greatest and most lasting gift they can give is one of faithful prayer. May each of us leave a lasting legacy to our grandchildren, one that will continue for generations to come—a legacy of prayer, love and spiritual influence. Let us be unwavering in our commitment to pray for our grandchildren's generation, and in our faith that they will in turn pray for the generations that come after them.

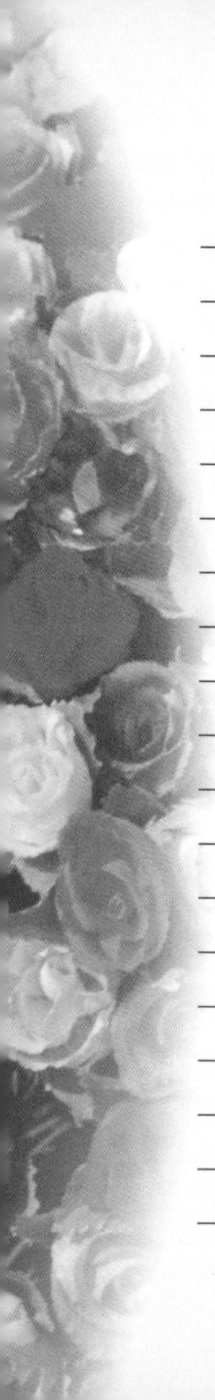

My Prayer for My Grandchildren

_____

_____

_____

_____

_____

_____

_____

_____

_____

_____

_____

_____

_____

_____

_____

_____

_____

_____

_____

_____

My Prayer for My Grandchildren

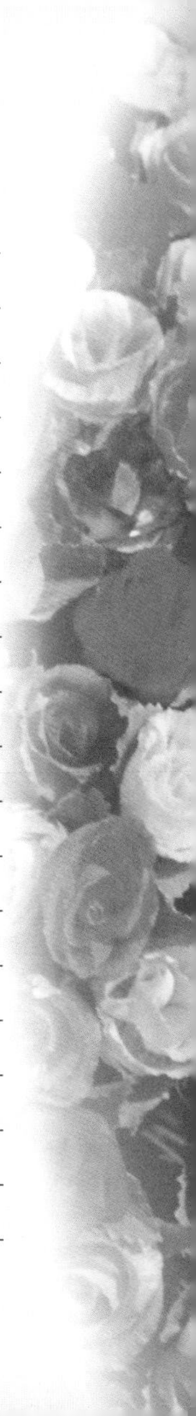

_____

_____

_____

_____

_____

_____

_____

_____

_____

_____

_____

_____

_____

_____

_____

_____

_____

_____

_____

_____

_____

_____

∽

Sources

Sherrer, Quin with Ruthanne Garlock, Adapted from *How To Pray For Your Children* © 1998 by Quin Sherrer, (Ventura, CA: Regal Books, 1998), Used with permission.

Smalley, Gary and John Trent, Ph.D, *The Blessing.* (Nashville, TN: Thomas Nelson, 1986).

Wilkinson, Bruce, *The Prayer of Jabez,* (Sisters, Oregon: Multnomah Publishers, 2000).

Sherrer, Quin and Ruthanne Garlock, Adapted from *Prayer Partnerships* (Ann Arbor, MI: Servant Publications, 2001).

Sherrer, Quin and Ruthanne Garlock, *Praying Prodigals Home*, (Ventura, CA: Regal Books, 2000), Used with permission.

I wish to acknowledge two special
people who made this book possible:
Molly Detweiler, my wonderful editor, and
Ann Spangler, my friend and agent.

Quin Sherrer

About the Author

Quin holds a bachelor's degree in journalism from Florida State University. She has written or co-authored twenty books for the Christian market, several of which have been best-sellers including *How to Pray For Your Children* and *A Woman's Guide To Spiritual Warfare*. Her latest book is *Grandma, I Need Your Prayers*. She's been a guest on more than two hundred radio or television shows, speaking on prayer and strengthening the family.

Her service on both the U.S. National and International board of directors for Women's Aglow Fellowship took her on speaking engagements to more than forty states and a dozen countries. She continues to speak at many weekend retreats for church and women's groups.

Quin's passion is to help teach Christians how to pray more effectively—basing their prayers on the Word of God.

In addition to writing, Quin babysits her six grandchildren frequently, imparting to them that God has a specific destiny for each of them—a plan and a purpose. The grandchildren range in age from seven months to seven years. She and her husband, LeRoy have been married for forty-six years and they pray together daily for their three adult children and their six grandchildren—all of whom now live nearby.